# Learning Bitcoin

Embrace the new world of fiance by leveraging
the power of crypto-currencies using Bitcoin and
the Blockchain

**Richard Caetano**

**[PACKT]** open source*
PUBLISHING      community experience distilled

BIRMINGHAM - MUMBAI

# Learning Bitcoin

First published: November 2015

Production reference: 1271015

Published by Packt Publishing Ltd.
Livery Place
35 Livery Street
Birmingham B3 2PB, UK.

ISBN 978-1-78528-730-5

www.packtpub.com

# Credits

**Author**
Richard Caetano

**Reviewers**
Francesco Canessa

Jose Celano

**Commissioning Editor**
Edward Bowkett

**Acquisition Editor**
Tushar Gupta

**Content Development Editor**
Dharmesh Parmar

**Technical Editor**
Namrata Patil

**Copy Editor**
Alpha Singh

**Project Coordinator**
Harshal Ved

**Proofreader**
Safis Editing

**Indexer**
Rekha Nair

**Production Coordinator**
Aparna Bhagat

**Cover Work**
Aparna Bhagat

# About the Author

**Richard Caetano** is an entrepreneur and software developer living in Paris, France, and was originally raised on a dairy farm in the middle of California. He discovered a strong interest in software development at an early age. Over the years, he has designed and developed systems ranging from agriculture process automation and government accounting to high-tech security, digital music, and mobile video games.

In 2011, Richard found the Bitcoin whitepaper and experienced a paradigm shift. After realizing the potential of this new technology, he changed course, and since then has been evangelizing this powerful new technology to the world.

He launched an early application called btcReport, which leverages good design to bring news and information to those interested in Bitcoin. Since then, he has been speaking at conferences and meetings to help spread the word about Bitcoin.

In 2015, he launched Stratumn, a company focused on helping developers build transparent, easy-to-audit, and secure applications by using the blockchain, the technology that powers the Bitcoin currency.

# Acknowledgments

I would like to first thank Tyler Love, a close friend from my hometown in California. I clearly remember the day, back in early 2011, when he sent me an instant message about Bitcoin. It has been an amazing journey since that day, and has been ever so rewarding.

I'm very thankful to my good friends at Epicenter Bitcoin, Sebastien Couture and Brian Fabian Crain, as they were the ones who introduced me to the publisher of Learning Bitcoin. In addition, I would like to thank all my friends in and around the Bitcoin space.

The editorial staff at Packt Publishing has been very supportive and helpful in making this book project a reality. I would like to thank Tushar Gupta for getting me into the right headspace to write, Natasha DSouza for her encouragement, Dharmesh Parmar for his guidance towards delivery, and Namrata Patil for her attention to the editorial details. I especially would like to thank the technical reviewers of the book: Francesco Canessa, Jose Celano, and John Jegutanis.

I have all my family and friends from my childhood on the farm to thank for all the opportunities I have had in life. I am thankful for my father's patience as he taught me electronics, and my mother's support as she took me to Radio Shack countless times to purchase packets of transistors and diodes. Ultimately, it was the TRS-80 computer that they gave me that set the course for my life.

I would like to mention Atelier Meraki located in my neighborhood in Paris. While writing this book, I spent many late nights working there. The word "Meraki" in Greek means to put your love, soul, and creativity into your work. That motto has been an inspiration for this project. I would like to thank Sherif Sy and Marie-Charlotte Moreau for all their hard work in making the space a wonderful place to work.

I would like to thank my Buddhist teachers and friends for helping me work with the best state of mind. More and more, I find that happiness comes from the simplest of lessons. Thank you.

Mais surtout, je tiens à remercier mon épouse Cécile pour toute son aide et son soutien alors que j'ai sauté la tête la première dans le Bitcoin. À l'époque, cela pouvait sembler une idée folle mais elle m'a toujours été derrière moi. C'est grâce à elle que j'ai écrit ce livre.

# About the Reviewers

**Francesco Canessa** is a software developer experienced in Bitcoin and blockchain technologies. His preferred tools when working with Bitcoin are Bitcoin Core via its JSON API for its solidity and simplicity, and the Bitcore JavaScript library for making slim client-side wallet software. As he believes that Bitcoin and blockchain are important innovations of our times, he builds open source projects (for example, BitNFC — `http://bitnfc.org`) to research and show the true power of these new technologies, and find new ways to drive Bitcoin's adoption. He has been working as the main translator on the Italian edition of *Mastering Bitcoin*, *O'Reilly Media*, written by Andreas M. Antonopoulous. His favorite programming language is Ruby and his hobbies are creating 3D printers and IoT.

**Jose Celano** started with computers when he was 10 and was given a Commodore 64. Jose holds a bachelor's degree in technical engineering in computer systems from the University of Las Palmas de Gran Canaria. He set up an IT company in 2004 after he finished his studies (iQ ingenieros), where he worked for 10 years, mainly developing web applications. He has always been interested in Internet payment systems and web development.

In September 2013, he began to investigate Bitcoin. In February 2014, he become a freelancer and started working on Bitcoin projects. Recently, Jose has worked as a private PHP consultant for BlockCypher, a San Francisco start-up providing blockchain web services to enable developers to easily build reliable blockchain applications.

# www.PacktPub.com

## Support files, eBooks, discount offers, and more

For support files and downloads related to your book, please visit www.PacktPub.com.

Did you know that Packt offers eBook versions of every book published, with PDF and ePub files available? You can upgrade to the eBook version at www.PacktPub.com and as a print book customer, you are entitled to a discount on the eBook copy. Get in touch with us at service@packtpub.com for more details.

At www.PacktPub.com, you can also read a collection of free technical articles, sign up for a range of free newsletters and receive exclusive discounts and offers on Packt books and eBooks.

https://www2.packtpub.com/books/subscription/packtlib

Do you need instant solutions to your IT questions? PacktLib is Packt's online digital book library. Here, you can search, access, and read Packt's entire library of books.

## Why subscribe?

- Fully searchable across every book published by Packt
- Copy and paste, print, and bookmark content
- On demand and accessible via a web browser

## Free access for Packt account holders

If you have an account with Packt at www.PacktPub.com, you can use this to access PacktLib today and view 9 entirely free books. Simply use your login credentials for immediate access.

# Table of Contents

# Preface

Bitcoin is truly a new kind of money. As an open network of computers, it exists purely on the Internet. Anyone with access to the Internet can send and receive money as easily as sending an e-mail. With this new form of digital cash, we are seeing the beginning of a new world of finance.

Bitcoin was launched in January 2009, just a few months after the financial crisis of 2008. As a true peer-to-peer currency, anyone in the world has access to bitcoin, with the ability to send it to anyone else. Its design insures that nobody can have their funds locked or taken away. The effects of this breakthrough currency are quite impressive. We have already seen the currency rise in price from less than one US cent to over a thousand dollars.

Since its launch, Bitcoin has challenged the mainstream view of finance. Originally designed as Digital Gold, Bitcoin's scarce supply and resistance to manipulation has resulted in an explosion of new ideas and projects with the strong potential to disrupt major industries and revolutionize finance.

Its anonymous creator, Satoshi Nakamoto, is only known through his contributions, namely the Bitcoin whitepaper and his initial forum posts to help guide core developers to support and maintain the source code. While nobody can confirm his identity, the value of his work is evident in the fact that the Bitcoin source code has been tested and challenged without any serious bugs or exploits reported. This is truly an amazing feat.

In this book, we will introduce Bitcoin with a hands-on approach. We will begin with a simple and easy-to-follow introduction, which includes buying and selling bitcoin. Throughout the middle, we will look into the internal workings of Bitcoin to understand how its various pieces work. Towards the end, we will explore various ways in which Bitcoin can be used as "programmable money".

# What this book covers

*Chapter 1*, *Setting Up a Wallet*, introduces the reader to Bitcoin and how to purchase some within 15 minutes. It covers the basics of Bitcoin, which includes addresses, keys, and wallets.

*Chapter 2*, *Buying and Selling Bitcoins*, covers more advanced ways of buying and selling bitcoin. Market trading and the tools involved are introduced.

*Chapter 3*, *Protecting Your Bitcoins*, educates you about how to become *your own bank*. Different approaches to safeguarding bitcoin are introduced and discussed.

*Chapter 4*, *Understanding the Blockchain*, gets into the nuts and bolts of Bitcoin's underlying technology. Its various technologies and algorithms are illustrated and explained.

*Chapter 5*, *Installing a Bitcoin Node*, is a step-by-step tutorial on setting up a Bitcoin node, which allows you to participate in the network. Some basic Bitcoin programming is introduced.

*Chapter 6*, *Understanding the Mining Process*, guides you through the various options available for mining bitcoin. The chapter focuses on the expenses involved and helps you to evaluate profitability.

*Chapter 7*, *Programming Bitcoin*, dives into the potential of Bitcoin as "programmable money". The chapter describes an example of how to build a simple Bitcoin escrow service using JavaScript.

*Chapter 8*, *Exploring Alternative Coins*, takes a tour around four innovative alternative coins based on Bitcoin's original source code. It ends with an example of how to set up a voting ballot secured by cryptographic proof.

# What you need for this book

To follow along with the examples of this book, you will need a modern web browser and a stable internet connection. Many of the Bitcoin services mentioned in the book are web-based and will only work on modern equipment. An iOS or Android smartphone might be necessary for some operations and authentication.

To be able to set up and install a Bitcoin node, a fast internet connection and a computer with a strong processor is required. The hard drive should have a minimum storage of 50 GB available, but more will be needed as the blockchain grows in size.

For the various aspects that involve programming, a computer with access to a terminal is required. Mac OS/X, Windows, and Linux have console access within a terminal. There are some additional tools required for setting up, such as Node.js, in order to follow along with the examples. Lists of the tools are provided with the examples.

If you are interested in setting up a Bitcoin mining rig, special equipment is required. Some of the equipment might be difficult to find and expensive to purchase. As the market is still new, one can expect many changes in pricing and availability. It is recommended that you check the forums and online marketplaces, such as eBay and Craigslist, to find more information about purchasing the equipment.

# Who this book is for

This book is written to help introduce Bitcoin to anyone who has basic experience with online banking. Most of the first half of the book is written for those who are very new to digital finance.

The second half of the book is written for those who are interested in seeing Bitcoin's potential. You do not have to be a programmer or hardware engineer to follow along, as simple explanations with clear illustrations are provided.

For more technical readers, scripts and installation notes are provided to help develop a deeper understanding of Bitcoin.

# Conventions

In this book, you will find a number of text styles that distinguish between different kinds of information. Here are some examples of these styles, and explanations of their meanings.

Code words in text, database table names, folder names, filenames, file extensions, pathnames, dummy URLs, user input, and Twitter handles are shown as follows: "We can include other contexts through the use of the `include` directive."

A block of code is set as follows:

```
// convert 'satoshi' to bitcoin value
var satoshiToBTC = function(value) {
  return value * 0.00000001
}
```

Any command-line input or output is written as follows:

```
~ npm install bitcoinjs-lib -g
```

New terms and important words are shown in bold. Words that you see on the screen, for example, in menus or dialog boxes, appear in the text like this: "Clicking the **Next** button moves you to the next screen."

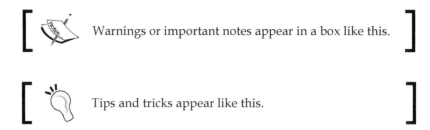

Warnings or important notes appear in a box like this.

Tips and tricks appear like this.

# Reader feedback

Feedback from our readers is always welcome. Let us know what you think about this book—what you liked or disliked. Reader feedback is important for us as it helps us develop titles that you will really get the most out of.

To send us general feedback, simply e-mail feedback@packtpub.com, and mention the book's title in the subject of your message.

If there is a topic that you have expertise in and you are interested in either writing or contributing to a book, see our author guide at www.packtpub.com/authors.

# Customer support

Now that you are the proud owner of a Packt book, we have a number of things to help you to get the most from your purchase.

# Downloading the example code

You can download the example code files from your account at http://www.packtpub.com for all the Packt Publishing books you have purchased. If you purchased this book elsewhere, you can visit http://www.packtpub.com/support and register to have the files e-mailed directly to you.

# Errata

Although we have taken every care to ensure the accuracy of our content, mistakes do happen. If you find a mistake in one of our books—maybe a mistake in the text or the code—we would be grateful if you could report this to us. By doing so, you can save other readers from frustration and help us improve subsequent versions of this book. If you find any errata, please report them by visiting `http://www.packtpub.com/submit-errata`, selecting your book, clicking on the Errata Submission Form link, and entering the details of your errata. Once your errata are verified, your submission will be accepted and the errata will be uploaded to our website or added to any list of existing errata under the Errata section of that title.

To view the previously submitted errata, go to `https://www.packtpub.com/books/content/support` and enter the name of the book in the search field. The required information will appear under the Errata section.

# Piracy

Piracy of copyrighted material on the Internet is an ongoing problem across all media. At Packt, we take the protection of our copyright and licenses very seriously. If you come across any illegal copies of our works in any form on the Internet, please provide us with the location address or website name immediately so that we can pursue a remedy.

Please contact us at `copyright@packtpub.com` with a link to the suspected pirated material.

We appreciate your help in protecting our authors and our ability to bring you valuable content.

# Questions

If you have a problem with any aspect of this book, you can contact us at `questions@packtpub.com`, and we will do our best to address the problem.

# 1
# Setting up a Wallet

*"When bitcoin currency is converted from currency into cash, that interface has to remain under some regulatory safeguards. I think the fact that within the bitcoin universe an algorithm replaces the functions of the government ...[that] is actually pretty cool."*

*– Al Gore, former Vice President of the United States*

Bitcoin's potential is quickly becoming apparent in the rapidly changing world of Internet finance. In just the few short years since its launch, we have seen an explosion of interest in this new, and somewhat mysterious, Internet money. Yet, several questions quickly come to mind: How does it work? Where does it come from? How do I buy it?

In this chapter, we will illustrate, in simple terms, most of what anyone new to Bitcoin will need to know to start. We will start by covering the following core topics:

- Buying your first bitcoin, in 15 minutes
- Explaining Bitcoin addresses
- Sending and receiving
- Private keys and wallets
- Transactions and confirmations
- Comparing Bitcoin wallets

# A brief history of money

Humans have been trading various forms of money for thousands of years. Many types of precious objects, acting as a *Medium of Exchange*, have been used. In the early ages, we traded grain, cattle, shells, and gems for other goods and services. This type of money, which we can touch and see, can be considered **Physical Money**.

As civilization progressed, so did our political systems. Eventually, sparse tribes and villages consolidated into kingdoms, states, and empires. Through the transformation, we saw our money shift into *Political Money*; money that's governed and issued by a central body such as the King, Emperor or, as in today's society, a Central Bank. State issued coins, bills, and notes, as well as taxation, regulation, and monetary policy — all emerged from this shift.

Today, Internet technology connects us directly to each other, opening a vast range of possibilities. By dissolving pre-existing physical and political boundaries, for the first time in history, the entire planet has access to the same information. This level of access is guaranteed by the Internet's decentralized design. Without a centralized hub, there is no single point of failure or control.

Satoshi Nakamoto, the creator of Bitcoin, leveraged this powerful network to implement a peer-to-peer (P2P) system for exchanging virtual cash. Built on a decentralized design and protected by powerful cryptography, this new type of money is no longer physical, yet resilient against corruption and manipulation.

No single group of individuals, including governments, banks, and corporations, control Bitcoin because all the peers are equal actors, participating through the same protocol. Its monetary policy is defined and self-regulated by its open network of computers. Thus, with Bitcoin we're seeing the emergence of a new phase of money. This P2P money is called cryptographic money or simply *Crypto-Currency*.

We're going to start exploring the world of Bitcoin by purchasing a small amount.

# Buying your first bitcoin in 15 minutes

Buying bitcoin is similar to buying foreign currencies. When an American lands in Paris, the fist thing he/she may need to do is exchange dollars for Euros. While at the airport, it's likely he/she will be able to fid a currency exchange to help. Just as there are many exchanges for exchanging government currencies, there are many exchanges for exchanging bitcoins.

Today there are markets for exchanging bitcoin with most of the world's major currencies. Most of them are online markets through which you can connect your bank account or credit card. There are some markets where the buyer and seller meet in person to exchange by hand. For the more technical users, private markets exist on chat forums where anonymous users trade with the other users based on their online reputation.

Of all the diverse ways to buy bitcoin, using a reputable online exchange may be the likely option for most users. Online exchanges generally operate similar to conventional online banking systems and are easy to set up.

We're going to buy 25 dollars worth of bitcoin using a credit card with an online exchange called Circle. In 2013, Circle was launched by a team competent in technology and finance. Additionally, they are registered as a money transmitter with FinCEN, a US government agency responsible for safeguarding the financial system from illicit use. For US citizens, they offer an instant exchange with a user-friendly wallet service. To buy bitcoins with Circle, you'll need the following:

* Valid photo ID
* A US home or business address
* A US bank account or credit card
* An iOS or Android smartphone
* 15 Minutes of free time

Buying and selling bitcoin on Circle is only available to users with a US address. As a registered money transmitter, Circle must follow standard banking practices such as Know your customer (KYC) and anti-money laundering laws (AML). These are the requirements to accept bank transfers from the US banking system.

Most European and Canadian customers can use Coinbase (`http://coinbase.com`) for direct wire transfers. We'll discuss buying and selling with Coinbase later in *Chapter 2, Buying and Selling Bitcoins*.

What's important to remember about Bitcoin is that the currency exists independently of any government's requirement for an individual's identity. Bitcoins can be exchanged with cash, hand-to-hand, thus by passing the registration process that we will describe in this chapter.

There are services such as **Local Bitcoins** (`http://localbitcoins.com`) where the users can buy and sell Bitcoin through direct exchange with the other users. While it is generally safe to do so, some users may be at risk from local regulations. It is important to research the local currency laws before transacting through these services, especially with large amount of cash.

# Signing up for a wallet – five minutes

To begin the signup process, open `http://circle.com` in your web browser and follow the **SIGN UP** links. You will be prompted to enter your First Name, your name, your Email address, and a password. After submitting your details, Circle will send you an e-mail verification. Simply follow the instructions provided. If you don't receive the email, check the spam folder of the email address you provided.

After verifying your email address, you'll be asked to enable *two-factor authentication* using your mobile phone. This security system uses a code sent via SMS or through Google Authenticator to allow access to your account and confirm irreversible actions, such as sending bitcoin. This helps make your account more secure by combining your password with something you physically hold, that is, your phone.

Finally, Circle will prompt you to provide two security questions. In case you lose your password, these questions will be asked before you can reset it.

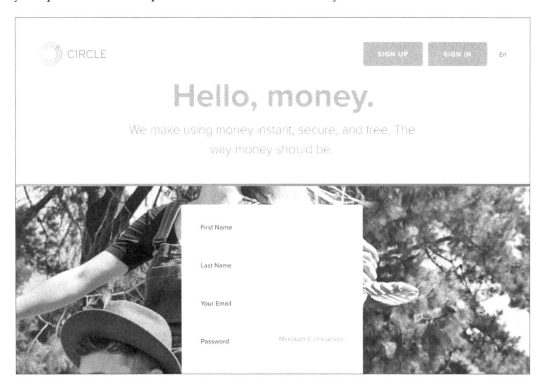

Figure 1.1 - Sign up with Circle to purchase bitcoin

# Adding a funding source – ten minutes

To purchase bitcoin, Circle requires a funding source. You can link a US bank account or a credit card. For this purpose, we will choose the credit card option as it's the quickest to set up.

 To meet Circle's KYC requirements, you'll need to submit a personal photo plus a scanned copy of your driver's license or passport.

1.  On the **ACCOUNT** page, which should show your balance as zero, click on the **Add Funds** button.

    Circle will prompt you to verify your mailing address along with your birth date and the last four digits of your social security number. This information is used to help verify your identification.

2.  Next, Circle will ask you to install their mobile application (available for iOS or Android). Using their mobile app, you'll be prompted to take a picture of yourself and your photo ID. Ensure that you arrange for proper lighting so that the image clearly shows the details of each digit. Once submitted, a confirmation will be given within a few minutes.

3.  If the app doesn't prompt you to verify your photo ID, you can manually upload the images. Open the mobile app under the **Account** table and click on the **Settings** icon. Under the **Settings**, click on **Link Accounts**. By following the instructions, you'll be prompted to upload the photos of your documents and credit card.

    At any stage, if you're experiencing issues, Circle offers support through online messaging. It also has toll free phone support for urgent issues.

4. After your identification has been verified, you're ready to add your credit card as a funding source. Return to your Circle account page and click on **Add Funds**. Circle will prompt you to enter your credit card information and will save it for future use.

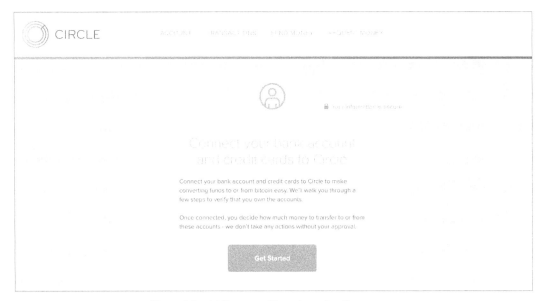

Figure 1.2 - Adding a credit card as a funding source

# Buying bitcoin – less than a minute

Once added, you're ready to buy bitcoin! Simply enter a dollar amount ($25 for our example), and review the bitcoin amount. You can preview and confirm any additional fees or charges below. Accepting the order will initiate an instant deposit to your online bitcoin wallet.

Figure 1.3 - Buy bitcoin instantly with Circle

# Looking at your Bitcoin balance

On your Circle account page, you can find the exact bitcoin balance under your dollar balance, as shown in the following figure:

Figure 1.4 - Your Bitcoin account and balance

Also indicated on your account page, under the balance, is the current USD to BTC exchange rate for Circle. The exchange rate can vary between services, depending on the supply and demand.

Also, in Figure 1.4, you can see that our account balance is currently $25.05, slightly higher that what we first purchased - $25.00 worth of bitcoin. This is due to a real time change in the exchange rate.

**IMPORTANT**

ONLY exchange money that's at your disposal. Bitcoin exchange rates can be quite volatile.

Bitcoin amounts are usually noted with the abbreviation BTC. This is similar to other currencies, such as USD and EUR. There are a few other symbols generally accepted by the Bitcoin community. Listed in the following table are the two most common ones:

| | |
|---|---|
| ฿ | First symbol used. Was released by early adopters and is available as an image. Only available as an image or through Font-Awesome. |
| B | Proposed by the community as an improvement to the original Bitcoin logo. Available on most devices as a standard Unicode character. |

Table 1 - Bitcoin currency logos

When expressing bitcoin amounts in plain text, using BTC is the easiest to type and universally accepted. However, if you would like to use the single character, check out Bitcoin Symbol (`http://bitcoinsymbol.org`) for more information on how to access the symbol.

On the account page shown in Figure 1.3, the exact Bitcoin balance account is presented as a decimal number:

0.10110406 BTC

Bitcoin amounts can have up to eight digits of precision. While every Bitcoin wallet must account for each digit of precision, the minimum amount that you can send may vary. Circle's minimum send amount is 0.00005460 BTC which is current with the amount proposed by the Bitcoin community.

Bitcoin units follow the standard metric system. The following prefixes can be used when expressing Bitcoin amounts:

| Unit | Abbreviation | Decimal |
|---|---|---|
| bitcoin | BTC | 1.0 |
| bitcent or centi-bitcoin | cBTC | 0.01 |
| millibit or milli-bitcoin | mBTC | 0.001 |
| bit or micro-bitcoin | µBTC | 0.000001 |
| satoshi | - | 0.00000001 |

Table 2 - Bitcoin abbreviations and units

Referring to the preceding table, you can write 0.44234 BTC as 442.34 mBTC. Some services and exchanges have adopted this format to make your account balance easier to read. Because amounts listed in whole numbers are generally easier to hold in one's mind, displaying the amounts in mBTC can be ideal. A cup of coffee at the time of this writing costs around 10mBTC.

The smallest unit of bitcoin, 0.00000001 BTC, is called a *Satoshi*, named after the developer of Bitcoin, Satoshi Nakamoto.

Some wallets allow you to change the unit of bitcoin presented in settings. This may make accounting and calculations easier, depending on your use case, especially if the exchange rate has many decimal places.

The accepted convention is to use Bitcoin (uppercase B) to refer to the technology and community, and bitcoin (lowercase) for the currency.

Do you have a Bitcoin wallet? I will send you 2.5 bitcoin.

# Explaining Bitcoin addresses

Similar to an email address, a Bitcoin address, or simply *address*, is used to receive and hold bitcoin. While people typically have one primary email address, Bitcoin users have many addresses. They are created at no cost by your Bitcoin wallet each time you request to receive money. Anyone with access to a Bitcoin wallet can create an unlimited number of addresses.

Bitcoin addresses usually have 26-35 characters and are case sensitive, as in the following example:

1MgErLiH1DuGMrd58fuL4CLQHc4VSboqKn

The address can contain numbers and letters, both uppercase and lowercase. To help reduce confusion, there are no capital O's, zeros 0's, lower case l's, and capital 'I's'. These characters are removed to reduce the errors made from writing with pen and paper, as often encountered in the past. The result is a format that is easy to share digitally and/or physically.

Bitcoin addresses have an error-checking code called a checksum. Computing the checksum of an address will detect if any single character is incorrect. This helps to prevent errors when sharing your address. Most wallets will validate and reject an invalid address. As an example, note the following two addresses:

- **Valid Bitcoin address**:

  1MgErLiH1DuGMrd58fuL4CLQHc4VSboqKn

- **Invalid Bitcoin address**:

  1MgErLiH1DuGMrd58fuL4CLQHc4VSboqKN

They both appear valid, yet the second address does not compute a valid checksum. They are nearly identical except for the uppercase N at the end of the second address.

 Checksums have been used in finance for many years. All credit card numbers have a built in checksum digit, specific to the issuing bank.

Your Bitcoin wallet will typically hold many Bitcoin addresses. It's important to know that a single Bitcoin address is not a wallet nor is it your account; rather, it's simply a way to receive money.

# Sending and receiving bitcoins

Your wallet's total spendable balance is a combination of the balances from all the Bitcoin addresses listed in the wallet. When spending bitcoins, the wallet is able to combine the balances of multiple addresses into one transaction.

It is important to note that Bitcoin was designed for its users to hold and manage their own keys. This makes it virtually impossible for another party to block, steal, or confiscate their money.

Intended as a gentle introduction to Bitcoin, this chapter introduces a centralized service, Circle, to help one get started with Bitcoin.

Circle's wallet service simplifies using Bitcoin by managing the addresses and private keys for you. This results in a clean *online banking*-like experience. However, it's important to realize that there is no requirement to use a service like Circle to store your bitcoins.

Later in the book, we will discuss how to manage your own wallet.

# Sending bitcoins

From your Circle account, simply click the **SEND MONEY** link from the menu above to access the send options. Circle offers two ways to send bitcoin. You can either send it to a Bitcoin address or an email address.

If you are sending it to an email address, Circle will check to see if the address has a valid account registered to it and make an instant deposit into that user's wallet. If the receiver is not registered, an invitation will be sent with instructions on how to set up an account.

Figure 1.5 - Send bitcoin from your Circle account

In the **To** field, simply enter the Bitcoin address or the email address of the user you'd like to pay. For the amount, you can specify either USD or BTC. If you enter an amount in USD, Circle will automatically calculate the exchange rate. Optionally, you can provide a memo to describe your transaction.

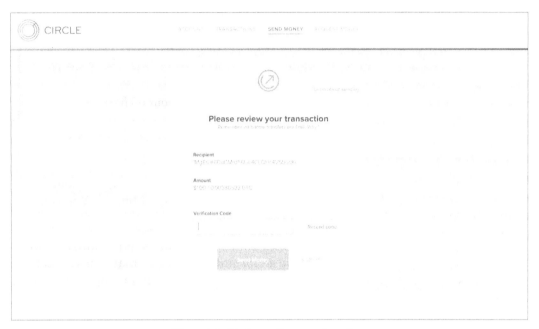

Figure 1.6 - Circle sending a confirmation

Continuing to the next step, Circle will prompt you to enter your two-factor authentication code. This code will be sent to your mobile phone. Using this two-factor authentication helps protect your wallet from unauthorized access.

Once submitted, your transaction will be recorded instantly.

For payments between two Circle users, the transaction will be confirmed immediately. Circle maintains an internal ledger and will record the transaction off the Bitcoin network.

Circle to Circle payments are called *off-chain* payments. *Chain* in this case refers to the Blockchain, the data structure used to store all the Bitcoin transactions. Off-chain means that a payment was recorded outside the Blockchain, using a private ledger.

For payments sent to a Bitcoin address, there will be a short period of time before the transaction is confirmed and accepted by the network. Generally, this takes about 10 minutes, but it can vary depending on the network's computing power.

You can review all your payments by clicking **TRANSACTIONS** from the main menu.

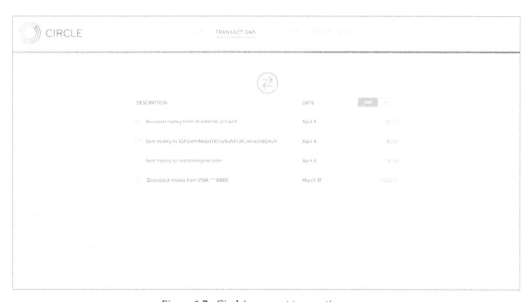

Figure 1.7 - Circle's account transactions page

# Receiving bitcoins

Circle provides two ways to receive bitcoin. Similar to sending bitcoin, you can send a request via email or share your Bitcoin address.

To start, click the **REQUEST MONEY** link from the main menu above. You'll be prompted to create a request:

Figure 1.8 - Requesting money

If you submit an email address, the recipient will receive an email providing them with instructions on how to pay. They will be given the following options:

- Sign into their Circle account and pay
- Open a new Circle account, fund it, and pay
- Pay with another service using a Bitcoin address

If you select the option to **Create an address and QR code**, Circle will generate a new Bitcoin address for you and present a QR code to scan. You can either copy/paste the address and share it with the sender, or allow them to scan the QR using a mobile device.

Figure 1.9 - Requesting money using a QR code

# Private keys and wallets

While Bitcoin addresses appear to be a string of random numbers, they are actually computed from a **private key**. Private keys are long strings of random characters generated by your Bitcoin wallet software. There can only be one address generated from your private key, thus your private key is both the seed and password to your Bitcoin address.

**IMPORTANT**

The private keys are normally hidden by your Bitcoin wallet, but they can be occasionally printed on paper as a physical backup. They should never be shared publicly as they control access to your funds.

Bitcoin private keys generally contain 51 characters and start with a 5, such as in the following example:

5Jd54v5mVLvyRsjDGTFbTZFGvwLosYKayRosbLYMxZFBLfEpCS7

Similar to your pocket wallet with credit cards, your Bitcoin wallet is a collection of addresses and private keys. Each address is used to receive and hold bitcoin.

| Bitcoin Address<br>Private Key | Bitcoin Amount |
|---|---|
| **12yuztN6Ci1p3h334YSKDFWWuexRtGu1f6**<br>5KgtRmuFSgqcjhiE4TLD1pPFvKVLbmfjyavrBwnGV5eW8eRgoKM | 3.14000000 |
| **1L3cM9UTdEtKVp5nMjgvdNr5wNyBon8kzB**<br>5HrfH1Za4kNEZFmhMe3LKwbztAScAGFkiGZqpq5aGigwX8vsSAh | 0.22340000 |
| **1EKMiayzXDbLFRVCiMZowewnHNvgWEet16**<br>5HrfH1Za4kNEZFmhMe3LKwbztAScAGFkiGZqpq5aGigwX8vsSAh | 1.22395800 |
| **1JWk1RG6hgbHCTv85eXvHWjCfebN64PHwV**<br>5JzquBknRfsyiynxjCSho4AWBfuT3nd5LfZxT9VRoq5NCsRcedd | 0.00398840 |
| Total wallet balance: | 4.59134640 |

Table 3 - Bitcoin addresses and private keys

In the preceding table, we can see how the balance in a typical wallet is composed of multiple Bitcoin addresses (in bold) with their corresponding private keys. Each address holds a balance that can be combined for a payout.

While most Bitcoin software holding your bitcoin are called wallets, they are technically **keychains**. Keychains are designed to manage and protect your Bitcoin keys. The term wallet is a convention carried over from Bitcoin legacy software.

**IMPORTANT**

It is not possible to recover lost private keys. If you choose to manage your own private keys, be sure that you're able to backup and restore them.

Due to the risk of loss, it should also be mentioned that online wallets are subject to the same risks. Without proper security and procedures, some online wallets have been hacked, resulting in losses.

Therefore, it is advisable to choose online services that have a good reputation and offer insurance against loss. Circle and Coinbase, mentioned later in the book, both carry insurance to help protect their customers from fraud and theft.

Reputable online wallets take the necessary precautions to protect your private keys. Most online wallets use a technique called **Cold storage**. Holding private keys in cold storage means that your keys are physically stored offline in a vault. Access to the vault is required to interact with the keys.

Additionally, *multi-signature addresses* are used to protect the coins in cold storage. Typically, an address will require one key to transfer its bitcoins. Multi-signature addresses usually require two or more keys to sign a transfer. With cold-storage, there will often be a two of three requirement so that no one employee has full access to the funds.

Private keys are generated from large amounts of random data, called **entropy** in computer science, and are very difficult to crack. With all the computing power available today, it is not possible to find the private key of a Bitcoin address using brute force methods. Even if computing power were to exponentially increase to the point where that's possible, the Bitcoin software can be upgraded to include new cryptographic methods to match.

# Transactions and confirmations

The Bitcoin network is essentially a public ledger that's able to record and validate millions of transactions. Transactions validated by the network are irreversible and impossible to change or alter. In this section, we're going to look at two core aspects of the network: transactions and confirmations.

# Transactions

A Bitcoin transaction is a record of a transfer between two or more bitcoin addresses. Similar to a credit or debit on your bank statement, the transaction records the sender, the receiver, and a date/time stamp.

All Bitcoin transactions are publicly accessible. However, the user's identify is never stored. Similar to a Swiss Bank account, only their public addresses are recorded. This makes it difficult to trace the address back to its owner. Therefore, we say that Bitcoin is pseudonymous.

Bitcoin has been used to fund illegal online markets, such as the Silk Road, with a special internet protocol call Tor. Using Tor allows the users to hide their computers' IP addresses, making it difficult to discover their physical location.

Using Tor, the users are able to place orders for illegal items. With payments made in Bitcoin and the shipping addresses encrypted, it is very difficult to link customers with their orders.

While Bitcoin's design hides the owner of an address, if an identity can be associated with a previous transaction, it can be possible to link a purchase with a user.

More flexible than a simple bank transfer, a Bitcoin transaction can withdraw from multiple addresses to pay a list of addresses. The transaction records every address used and must account for the full balance. Any unspent bitcoin must be sent back to a "change address". It works like paying for an item that costs 12 dollars with two 10 dollar bills. The merchant accepts the two bills and returns 8 dollars in change.

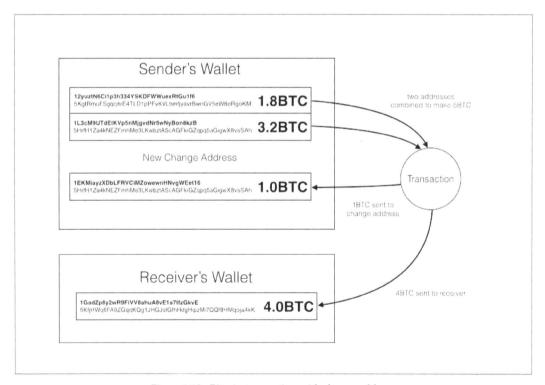

Figure 1.10 - Bitcoin transaction with change address

In Figure 1.10, we show a starting balance of 5BTC between two addresses in our bitcoin wallet. We then send 4BTC to the receiver. To account for the full balance, the transaction returns 1BTC to our *change address*. After the transaction, the two funding addresses will contain 0BTC each.

The change address is optional as we can reuse an existing bitcoin address. However, most wallets create a new address as it's recommended to increase your privacy.

Before sending a transaction to the Bitcoin network for confirmation, it must be signed with the private keys of the input addresses listed. Similar to your bank requiring your signature on a check, the Bitcoin network requires you to sign your transaction before confirming it.

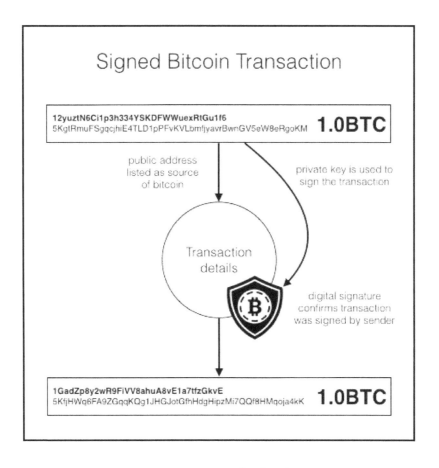

Figure 1.11 - A transaction with a digital signature

Bitcoin uses a digital signature to sign your transaction. The signature can only be generated by the holder of the private key. Illustrated in Figure 1.9, we can see how this signature is created and stored in the transaction.

The digital signature is used by the network to verify that the transaction was created by someone who has access to the private key. Without this verification, the transaction would be rejected from the public ledger.

The process of computing the digital signature is handled automatically by your Bitcoin wallet. The digitally signed transaction is now ready for confirmation by the network. We will discuss digital signatures in detail later in *Chapter 4, Understanding the Blockchain*.

> Bitcoin wallet software is designed to handle the complexities of sending/receiving bitcoin. The example is given here to help deepen our understanding of how transactions work.

## Confirmations

After it's digitally signed, the transaction is broadcasted to the Bitcoin network and reviewed by many nodes on the network. Each node is essentially a computer with a copy of the ledger, with access to all the transactions since the beginning. The node's job is to listen for new transactions and relay them to the other nodes on the network.

Some nodes serve as *miners*. Miners perform computational work to ensure that each transaction is valid that it does not double the, or spend more than the available. Each miner must then prove the results to the other miners. Any discrepancies will cause the network to reject a miner's results.

> Miners have a financial incentive to do this work. Along with confirming the transactions, there is a cryptographic puzzle to solve. If the miner can prove their solution, they are awarded new Bitcoins and/or transaction fees. The solution to the puzzle is called **proof-of-work**.

This process is what makes the Bitcoin network both resilient and trustworthy. The larger the network of miners with consensus, the more we can trust the validity of the ledger. This is how Satoshi was able to design a network for exchanging virtual cash without a single point of control or failure.

Unconfirmed transactions start with zero confirmations. When a miner's work is accepted by the network, the number of confirmations for each transaction is incremented by one. Confirmations are generally accepted every 10 minutes but can vary depending on the various computational aspects of the network.

As more miners confirm the results of the previous miners, the number of confirmations for your transaction continues to increase. After some time, your transaction can have hundreds or even thousands of confirmations. With such a large number of confirmations, you can be assured that your transaction cannot be reversed.

[  The more confirmations your transaction has, the more difficult it is to break, or hack. Mathematically speaking, a total of six confirmations is accepted as unchangeable but as few as one confirmation is sufficient for most small transactions. ]

The Bitcoin network is a very powerful network, especially when there is a large number of miners working together to validate and confirm the transactions on a public ledger. The entire ledger is copied by new miners joining the network. Transactions confirmed by an increasing number of miners results in more trust in the network. This design creates redundancy to guard against transaction fraud. Once a transaction is confirmed in the ledger, it cannot be deleted or changed.

Now that we have a basic understanding of how Bitcoin works, let's look at some wallet services and compare their differences.

# Comparing Bitcoin wallets

We have been using Circle as an online wallet to help make the introduction to Bitcoin gentler and safer. Yet there are other options we can use for sending and receiving Bitcoin. Each option has its advantages and disadvantages. Let's briefly discuss them now.

# Online wallets

Services such as Circle are called *online wallets*. Online wallets are web-based services that manage and store a small amount of your Bitcoins on a public web server. The rest are stored offline in a physical vault. They generally have the following characteristics:

- Available through a web browser or mobile application
- Create and store your private keys online
- Offer the option to send/receive via email address

- Have a built-in exchange to buy/sell bitcoin
- Offer quick and easy account signup
- Can be secured via two-factor authentication
- May offer insurance for loss of coins

While these are nice features to offer the public, some of the more proficient users are not in favor of having an organization control their funds.

In the past, some exchanges have suffered security breaches. While some of the services were able to cover the losses, others were not solvent and were unable to reimburse its users. That resulted in many users losing their funds.

When choosing an online wallet, be sure to do your research on the company, the team, and its history.

| Service | Description |
|---|---|
| **Circle**<br>`http://circle.com` | Great user experience, offers insurance and mobile application |
| **Coinbase**<br>`http://coinbase.com` | Offers many additional features, merchant tools, a mobile app, and full exchange |
| **Xapo**<br>`http://xapo.com` | Great user experience, strong offline storage, and Bitcoin debit card |
| **CoinKite**<br>`http://coinkite.com` | Online wallet with a Bitcoin payment terminal and debit card |
| **ANXPro**<br>`http://anxpro.com` | Online wallet, offers debit card in USD/EUR/GBP |

Table 3 - Online wallets

# Desktop wallets

For users who would like more control over their bitcoin, *desktop wallets* may be a better choice than online wallets.

Desktop wallets are applications that run on your computer and connect directly to the Bitcoin network. Having the application installed locally gives the users full control of their Bitcoin wallet and their private keys.

Some desktop wallets, such as Bitcoin Core, download a full copy of the Bitcoin ledger to disk. This can require more than 10 gigabytes of local storage and can take a couple of days to download and verify.

More efficient desktop wallets, called *lightweight clients*, connect to an online copy of the ledger. This reduces the storage requirements and the setup time. In most cases, your wallet can be ready within a few minutes.

The risk of using a desktop wallet includes hardware failures, computer viruses, and unauthorized access. Before accepting any Bitcoin to your desktop wallet, you should be familiar with the backup and restore process, and you must ensure that your computer is safe from malicious attacks.

For more advanced users, many desktop wallets offer a console where they can interact with their wallet by issuing commands. Users can generate various kinds of transactions and directly manipulate their list of private keys and addresses.

| Service | Description |
|---|---|
| **MulitBit**<br>`http://multibit.org` | Lightweight client, easy to set up for non-technical users. |
| **Bitcoin/QT**<br>`https://bitcoin.org` | Official Bitcoin desktop wallet. Downloads a full copy of the Bitcoin ledger. Discussed later in the book. |
| **Electrum**<br>`http://electrum.org` | Full featured desktop wallet. Synchronizes with an online service for quick ledger setup. |
| **Armory**<br>`https://bitcoinarmory.com` | Offers advanced features such as cold storage. |

Table 4 - Desktop wallets

In *Chapter 5, Installing a Bitcoin Node*, we'll explain how to safely use and configure Bitcoin Core, the official Bitcoin client, as a desktop wallet.

# Mobile wallets

Having access from your mobile phone is a practical way to carry and spend bitcoins on the go. Most of the online services mentioned previously have applications available for download on the iPhone and Android app stores. Because the Bitcoin keys are stored and managed on servers, your account is protected by your username and password.

 To increase the security of bitcoins stored on a mobile device, make sure to setup a PIN code for unlocking the phone.

It's also worth mentioning that there are independent mobile wallets that store access to the keys on the phone. Because storing the private keys on your phone can be risky, in the event it's lost or stolen, the wallets offer a way to protect your bitcoin with 24 words that are randomly chosen. You will be able to restore your wallet, if lost, using the passphrase.

| Service | Description |
|---------|-------------|
| **Breadwallet**<br>`http://breadwallet.com` | Well designed standalone mobile wallet and open source. |
| **Coinomi**<br>`https://coinomi.com` | A lightweight wallet that supports multiple languages, alt-currency exchanges, and is open sourced. |
| **Mycelium**<br>`https://mycelium.com` | Popular mobile wallet for Android. Accompanying application, Local trader, offers trading bitcoins hand-to-hand. |

Table 5 - Mobile wallets

# Hardware wallets

As one of the most secure options, *hardware wallets* store and encrypt your private keys on removable USB devices. Because the keys are never copied to your computer or made available online, it makes it extremely difficult to hack.

During setup, the hardware wallet will generate 24 random words, similar to the mobile wallets, as the password to your bitcoin. Backing up your wallet is as simple as backing up the list of words. To restore your device, you simply provide the same set of words during setup.

The two commercially available hardware wallets are Ledger (`https://www.ledgerwallet.com/`) and Trezor (`www.bitcointrezor.com`). They both plug into your USB port and include a user-friendly interface.

Wallets that use a 24-word passphrase implement a type of keychain, called a Hierarchical Deterministic Wallet, or HD Wallet. This type of keychain can produce an unlimited number of private keys and addresses, just from a master seed which is generated from the 24 random words. We will cover HD Wallets later in the book.

# Summary

In this chapter, we covered some of the basics of getting started with Bitcoin. We walked through a simple tutorial of how to buy bitcoin instantly and discussed addresses, private keys, and transactions. With this understanding, you can safely transact using Bitcoin.

In the next chapter, we will dive deeper into buying and selling. We will cover how to track prices for various currencies and how to trade bitcoin through an online exchange.

# 2
# Buying and Selling Bitcoins

*"I really like Bitcoin. I own Bitcoins. It's a store of value, a distributed ledger. It's a great place to put assets, especially in places like Argentina with 40 percent inflation, where $1 today is worth 60 cents in a year, and a government's currency does not hold value. It's also a good investment vehicle if you have an appetite for risk. But it won't be a currency until volatility slows down."*

*– David Marcus, CEO of Paypal*

Building on the basics that were introduced in *Chapter 1*, *Setting up a Wallet* we're going to set up a trading account with an online Bitcoin exchange. In this chapter, we're going to cover the following topics:

- Understanding Bitcoin's price volatility
- Following exchange rates and news
- Comparing Bitcoin exchanges
- Trading Bitcoins on an exchange
- Physical Bitcoins

## Understanding Bitcoin's price volatility

In May of 2010, the first significant Bitcoin transaction was exchanged. A pizza worth roughly $25 was purchased for 10,000 bitcoin. At today's pricing, where a single bitcoin is worth about $250, the same amount of bitcoin would be worth approximately $2,500,00. In retrospect, it was a "worthy" pizza!

Since then, Bitcoin's volatile price movements took the exchange rate, in US dollars, up to $1200 in 2013 and back down to $180 in 2015. It's quite an impressive history for a currency that's only six years old.

Before investing your own money in Bitcoin, it's advisable to become familiar with the reputable services available, as well as its price history. Linking significant events and stories to the price is a fundamental approach to trading bitcoin.

Compared to most other global markets, Bitcoin has an overall low volume. Thus, a large move by a big player can alter the price very quickly. Make sure to assess your personal financial risk level before investing any large amount of money in Bitcoin.

# Exchange rates

The first exchange rates for Bitcoin were calculated and published in October of 2009. It was a simple calculation that divided one US dollar by the average cost needed to mine a single bitcoin. The first rate published was approximately 1,300BTC for 1USD.

The first Bitcoin exchange rate was published on the "New Liberty Standard":

"During 2009 my exchange rate was calculated by dividing $1.00 by the average amount of electricity required to run a computer with high CPU for a year, 1331.5 kWh, multiplied by the average residential cost of electricity in the United States for the previous year, $0.1136, divided by 12 months, divided by the number of bitcoins generated by my computer over the past 30 days." http://newlibertystandard.wikifoundry.com/page/2009+Exchange+Rate ."

Today the free market determines the price of Bitcoin. Factored into the price by the market are many elements that include government reactions to Bitcoin, price rallies, adoption announcements, and investor speculation. Occasionally, the exchange rates have experienced sharp gains followed by steep losses, sometimes prompting the news media to make extreme or exaggerated claims, such as "Bitcoin is dead".

Yet, despite all the excitement from the ups and downs of trading, the Bitcoin network continues to operate independently of its trading price. We're truly seeing the digital version of gold standing on its own.

Similar to most commodities, Bitcoin's exchange rate can be listed in many different currencies, such as US dollar and Euro, as well as in its price against some commodities such as gold and silver.

To get a better feel for its current exchange rate, let's quickly highlight the major pricing events in its six years of history.

# Bitcoin's price history

Available on many exchanges, we can find a price chart showing Bitcoin's exchange rate since its beginning. The following chart, available at `https://blockchain.info/charts`, shows Bitcoin's price history in US dollars since 2009:

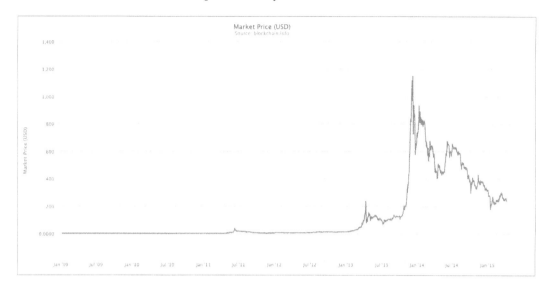

Figure 2.1 - Bitcoin's price history (source Blockchain.info)

For the first two and half years of Bitcoin's existence, its price remained less than one US dollar. The new digital currency was being mined quite easily at the time. With little mining competition, it was common for miners to earn 50 BTC a day.

Once parity with the dollar was reached, early in the year 2011, the mainstream news outlets started covering Bitcoin. Rapid growth and adoption soon followed, leading to much more competition for mining Bitcoin. The result was a quick boom in price.

Referring to the preceding market chart, let's review some key drivers that influenced significant changes in the Bitcoin price.

# Price bubbles

In market economics, a **bubble** is a cycle characterized by a rapid expansion or rise in price followed by a sharp correction. The changes in the market prices during a bubble are often unsupported by the underlining fundamentals, thus leading to the "post bubble crash". Over speculation is often the primary driver of bubbles.

In Figure 2.1, we can identify three significant price bubbles, with each having the characteristic rapid rise and fall in price.

The first bubble occurred circa July 2011. This is when the news media first picked up on Bitcoin. At the time, the USD/BTC exchange rate was around $2-3. Soon after, the price surpassed $30 in only a few weeks. Before the end of the year, the exchange rate fell back down to $2.

The next major bubble happened around April 2013. At that time, Bitcoin adoption was increasing and more people were familiar with it. At the same time, the government of Cyprus announced an unprecedented bailout of its banks. These were the conditions for a bubble that took the Bitcoin price to over $260. After the bubble, the price settled back down to around $140.

The largest bubble shown in the preceding price chart happened in late 2013 when the Chinese market exploded. With a large surge in interest in Bitcoin by the Chinese investors, the price surged past $1100 in a short period of time. The government officials responded by banning its banks from handling bitcoin transaction. Its citizens were not restricted from buying/selling Bitcoin, but without a legal framework for exchanges, fear dominated the markets. Less than 12 hours after the news was published, the exchange rate fell below $600. Uncertainty of government acceptance and restricted access to capital quickly cooled the surge in price.

Instability with government currencies may be one of the most significant drivers of Bitcoin price movements. As we've seen in the two largest bubbles, investors are looking for an alternative market, outside the restrictions imposed by the financial system. As governments' acceptance of Bitcoin can be quite uncertain, trading on these conditions can be quite risky.

Over time, as the Bitcoin market matures, we may eventually see price stability, but it's evident that it may take some time to get there. Until then, we can continue to see the price volatility tied with major global events and government acceptance.

# Theft

In the first few years of existence, many homebuilt websites were being used to provide Bitcoin services to the public. Bitcoin wallets and exchanges were being built quickly by enthusiasts. Yet, without experience in security, there were many thefts resulting in thousands of lost bitcoins.

In most of the cases, the Bitcoin theft was due to systems built with weak protection from invasion and/or exploitation in the software. Additionally, some services stored their full Bitcoin balance on public-facing servers. Best practices for storing customers' Bitcoin mandate that only a small portion of the full balance should be stored in an online *hot wallet*, with the remainder backed up on an offline *cold storage* wallet.

As the price started to increase over time, the public's reaction to theft became more sensitive. Many were still questioning Bitcoin's resilience to hacking with a component of confusion around what was actually getting hacked. The public was uncertain as to how safe it was to hold bitcoin. This uncertainty led to questioning Bitcoin's viability as a mainstream currency, leading to a decline in price. Eventually, as the public's understanding of Bitcoin was corrected, the price stabilized.

# Seizure

The Silk Road online drug market bust was the largest seizure of Bitcoin to date by government officials. Silk Road operated as a marketplace for illegal items such as drugs and weapons. At its height, more than 10,000 items, ranging from cannabis to heroin and from knives to pistols, were listed for sale, all priced in bitcoin.

Using an open sourced service called Tor, users were able to log in to the site anonymously and purchase items using Bitcoin. Using Tor with Bitcoin makes it very difficult to trace the connection between buyers and sellers. Thus, illegal sales flourished. It is estimated that, in 2013, Silk Road grossed $1.2 billion in revenue and earned $80 million in commissions.

**Dead Pirate Roberts** was the operator of Silk Road. Working anonymously, he inadvertently leaked enough traces of his identity that the DEA and the Secret Service were able to make an arrest. In October of 2013, Ross Ulbricht was arrested on charges of drug trafficking and money laundering.

Seizure of Bitcoin by law enforcement agencies resulted in some significant price movements. With the seizure of 144,000 bitcoin from the Silk Road bust, the traders were uncertain of Bitcoin's ability to sustain its price. This news resulted in a drop from $123 to $75. Two days later, the price recovered to around $118.

# Following exchange rates and news

To help track what's going on in the Bitcoin space, we'll look at some products and services to track exchange rates and related news events.

## Price tickers

There are many services that track and display Bitcoin exchange rates. One of the easiest apps to use is **btcReport** (available for iOS on the App Store):

Figure 2.2 - btcReport, a Bitcoin price ticker for the iPhone

The main display of btcReport, as shown in Figure 2.2, shows the latest trading price and news. Daily metrics are shown as changes in today's price (shown on the top), a ticker chart, and the trailing 3-day average (shown under the chart). Displayed along the bottom is a selection of currencies, and on the top right there is an option to change the exchange. btcReport functions nicely as an app in your pocket for a quick glance at the exchange price and recent movements.

For most users who wish to casually buy and sell bitcoin, btcReport offers a clean and uncluttered view into the markets.

The following table lists some other popular ticker apps suitable for the mainstream audience:

| Service | Platform | Description |
|---|---|---|
| **btcReport**<br>`btcreport.com` | iOS, Web | Clean and simple design. Supports price alerts and the largest list of currencies and markets. |
| **Coin Desk**<br>`coindesk.com` | Web, iOS, Android | Daily news articles and well organized price data for USD, EUR, GBP, and CNY. |
| **XBT Apps**<br>`xbtapps.com` | Android, iOS, Web | Works on Android. Supports price alerts and 29 exchanges. |
| **Bitcoin Wisdom**<br>`bitcoinwisdom.com` | Web | Candlestick charts and detailed pricing information. Great for advanced traders. |
| **Preev**<br>`preev.com` | Web | Very simple Bitcoin price converter. |

Table 1 - Bitcoin ticker apps

Bitcoin prices are also available from Google. Google stores and tracks historical Bitcoin price information and makes it available through their search engine. The following search terms are examples of how to access Google's pricing information from the search box:

**btc to usd**

**Bitcoin price in dollars**

As shown next in figure 2.3, Google offers a quick way to find the latest Bitcoin price. It displays a quick chart and offers a quick currency converter.

Figure 2.3 - Google's Bitcoin price chart

# Detailed price tracking

For those trading bitcoin on a more frequent basis, a more advanced and detailed view of the Bitcoin price is necessary. Many applications and services, which provide detailed price charts and analysis, are available to help the traders.

TRADING BITCOIN CAN BE RISKY. Market trading is well beyond the scope of this book. Learning Bitcoin's goal is to familiarize its readers with transacting in Bitcoin, including online trading.

If you're interested in learning more about trading for profit, please make sure you do proper research online, or through other sources of information on market trading and price chart analysis.

Shown in the following figure 2.3 is a service called **BitcoinWisdom**, available at `https://bitcoinwisdom.com/`:

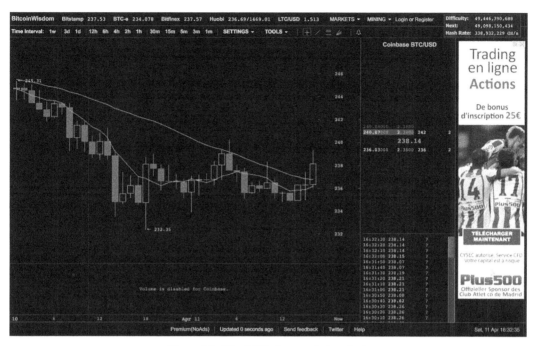

Figure 2.4 - BitcoinWisdom market analysis

BitcoinWisdom offers a more detailed look and analysis of the moving market prices. Each section of the screen displays detailed:

- Candle stick chart, shown in the main section
- Open market orders, shown to the right of the candlestick chart
- Last orders traded, shown below the open market orders section

# Candlestick charts

Market charts often display candlestick charts, which are dense with information. Each candlestick contains a bar, called the **body**, with a line both above and below, called the **wick**. The top of the body represents the open price, and the bottom, the close price. The wick extending above the body shows the high price and the one extending below shows the low price.

Each candle stick can represent an interval of time. The available intervals on BitcoinWisdom are shown along the top: 1w, 3d, 1d, 12h, 6h, and so on. The color, usually green or red, represents the movement of the price.

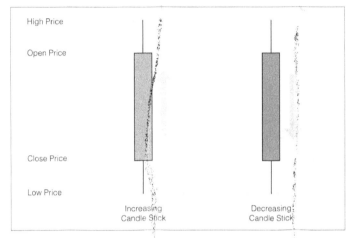

Figure 2.5 - Candle stick chart explanation

# Market orders

Online exchanges match buy or sell orders with their respective parties. The traders submit an order, listed as buy or sell, with the quantity and price. The orders sit in a queue called the **order book**. The order book lists all the buy and sell orders by amount, and is updated in real time. Usually, there is a gap between the highest buy order and the lowest sell order. The difference is called the **spread**.

Once an order is matched, it is recorded and displayed below the order book (refer to figure 2.4). Each order matched is then summarized and plotted as a candlestick chart. Moving averages are calculated and overlaid as a blue and yellow line.

# Trading techniques

There are primarily two ways to analyze market trading data: fundamental analysis and technical analysis.

Fundamental analysis is based on the underlying support of each market and stock or commodity. The company's assets, revenue, and profitability, as well as the associated economic environment, are all factored into the fundamental analysis. For example, Warren Buffet, one of the most famous investors, relies on the company's fundamentals before making an investment. These fundamentals are cited as his reasoning to invest in industries such as railroads and energy.

Technical analysis deals more with the day-to-day price movement. It factors in the psychological aspects of trading. Technical price analysis has the following guiding principles:

- The price reflects all known information
- Price action is more important than the news, earnings, and so on
- The market's price movement is based on emotions such as fear and greed
- Markets fluctuate and the actual price may not reflect its actual value

Candlestick charts are used extensively in technical analysis. The size of the body, the length of the wicks, and the movement of the price are all used to influence how to place trades.

Just to give an example of how to read candlestick charts, let's consider the body length given in a typical chart:

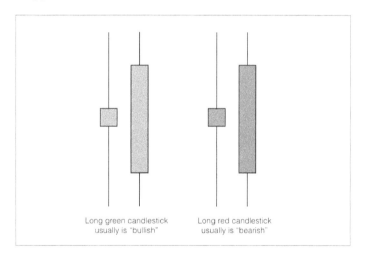

Figure 2.6 - Long green versus long red candlesticks

Long green candlesticks usually indicate strong buying pressure. The longer the wick, the further the close price is above the open price. Long green candlesticks can be found after an extended decline, marking a potential turning point or a resistance level.

Long red candlesticks usually indicate strong selling pressure. The longer the wick, the further the close price is below the open price. Long red candlesticks can be found after a long advance, indicating a turning point or a future resistance level.

In this chapter, we're providing a quick introduction to candlestick charts. In-depth coverage, with a broad range of examples of candlestick charts and technical analysis, can be found through online search.

**IMPORTANT**

Before beginning to day trade, it is extremely important to understand each market's particular dynamics and have some understanding of technical analysis. Remember to only trade with money that is at your disposal.

# News sources

Access to the latest news is very helpful for following trends and activity in the Bitcoin space. Quality news articles are available through several sources. Google provides a clean interface which combines historical price charts with the latest news.

Figure 2.7 - Google's finance page for Bitcoin

Google's finance page for Bitcoin displays price tracking alongside the latest news. You can easily access this information through Google's search bar, with the following terms:

**CURRENCY: BTC**

```
http://www.google.com/finance?q=CURRENCY:BTC
```

CoinDesk is a service focused on providing an in-depth look at the Bitcoin space. They publish daily news articles focusing on the latest developments, the exchange rate information, as well as a quarterly **State of Bitcoin** report.

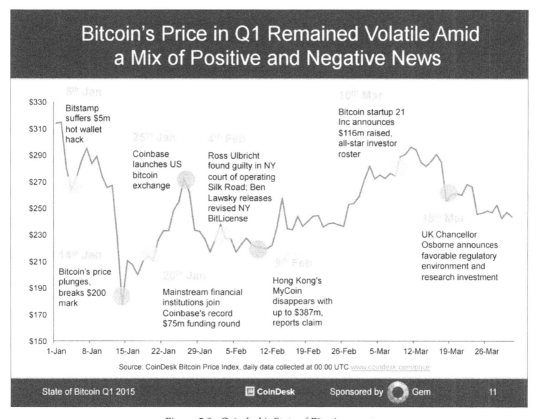

Figure 2.8 - Coindesk's State of Bitcoin report

The State of Bitcoin reports focus on the major events and drivers in the Bitcoin space. Researching these reports, on a quarterly basis, will help develop a better understanding of the *fundamentals* backing Bitcoin.

CoinDesk publishes several other periodicals related to Bitcoin. These reports can be found at `http://www.coindesk.com/bitcoin-reports`.

Listed in the following table are some of the sources of high-quality Bitcoin news and content:

| Service | Description |
|---|---|
| **CoinDesk**<br>`coindesk.com` | Offers a quarterly State of Bitcoin report and a detailed price history for the major markets |
| **The Coin Telegraph**<br>`cointelegraph.com` | Offers the latest news, prices, breakthroughs, and analysis with emphasis on expert opinion, and commentary from the digital currency community |
| **Bitcoin Magazine**<br>`bitcoinmagazine.com` | Periodical magazine that covers current events in business, technology, politics, law, and society |

Table 2 - Services offering Bitcoin-related news

# Comparing Bitcoin exchanges

Shortly after Bitcoin's beginning in 2009, online exchanges were created to facilitate buying and selling of Bitcoin. In 2010, MtGox was the first exchange to bring Bitcoin to the market. MtGox was originally a site for trading Magic the Gathering cards but was adapted for trading bitcoin. They grew quickly, both in user base and trade volume, and brought Bitcoin to many thousands of people. However, they were unable to sustain the pace of growth and met difficulty in meeting government compliance. Ultimately, they experienced a significant bitcoin theft that left them insolvent. In early 2014, they publicly announced their insolvency and filed bankruptcy.

Thus, when choosing a Bitcoin exchange, it's most important to do some research on the company and its operations. Let's cover some important aspects used to make a worthy comparison.

## Volume and liquidity

Consider an exchange with a light trading volume. If a large order is placed that exceeds the order book's capacity, the price can significantly change. To absorb a large order, a marketplace must be able to cover the order without a major change in price.

A marketplace's ability to process such orders is dependent on its *liquidity*. Depending on your trading requirements, some exchanges may not suffice. You can check the exchange's 30 day volume to get a picture of its liquidity.

# Fees and commissions

Most online Bitcoin exchanges charge a commission, both from the buyer and the seller, for each trade completed. The fees usually run between 0.1 percent and 0.5 percent, depending on the trading volume of the user. The rates are calculated on your total monthly volume and are often tiered to encourage volume trading.

For example, Bitstamp (`www.bitstamp.net`) charges fees based on your 30-day USD volume. To illustrate the fee structure, refer to the following table:

| Fee % | 30-day USD volume |
|---|---|
| 0.25% | < $20,000 |
| 0.24% | < $100,000 |
| 0.22% | < $200,000 |
| 0.20% | < $400,000 |
| 0.15% | < $600,000 |
| 0.14% | < $1,000,000 |
| 0.13% | < $2,000,000 |
| 0.12% | < $4,000,000 |
| 0.11% | < $20,000,000 |
| 0.10% | > $20,000,000 |

Table 3 - Bitstamp's fees based on trading volume

Coinbase Exchange (`https://exchange.coinbase.com/`) offers a different model for commission. It's based on a **taker/maker** schema. **Makers** are the orders that add liquidity to the exchange and **takers** are the orders that remove the liquidity. For example, if you place an order on the order books, you're a maker. If you place an order to purchase an existing order, you're a taker. Coinbase simply charges a 0.25 percent fee to all the takers and a 0.0 percent fee to all the makers.

# Transfer limits

Exchanges are subject to limits imposed by their banking partners and/or government regulations. For example, Coinbase has daily and monthly withdrawal limits based on your level of account verification. You may experience varying withdrawal limits, depending on the exchange policy.

For larger institutional investments, online Bitcoin exchanges may not carry sufficient liquidity. Currently emerging are privately managed Bitcoin funds and **electronically traded funds** (**ETF's**). A Bitcoin fund may purchase and securely hold a specified amount of Bitcoin. Shares representing a portion of the fund are then sold and traded. Privately managed Bitcoin funds may be more suitable for institutional investors to serve larger investments without exceeding the liquidity of an exchange's order book. Additionally, the bitcoins are securely held, relieving the investor of having to manage their storage.

# Jurisdiction and regulations

Bitcoin exchanges that accept transfers between the banking systems must get registered and comply with their local laws and regulations. Governments' licensing requirements often vary between jurisdictions, depending on the financial services offered. Therefore, it is important that any exchange that you do business with meets these requirements.

Some governments are not certain on how to classify Bitcoin. In the United States, the IRS classifies Bitcoin as a commodity subject to capital gains tax, while **FinCEN** treats it as a currency. These classifications are subject to change in line with Bitcoin adoption within governments.

Some banks are not able to accept the uncertainty of the ambiguity surrounding Bitcoin compliance. As a result, there have been several cases where an exchange's banking partner has discontinued business. This can often lead to slow withdrawal rates and service interruptions. Make sure to research the exchange's banking partnerships and their history of doing business together.

Any trader should consult with a tax professional to ensure they are in compliance with their local and state tax laws.

# Service uptime

An exchange's service uptime and capacity to handle peak loads of traffic are an important aspect to consider when choosing a Bitcoin exchange. Heavy trading excitement can lead to a spike in traffic, resulting in a heavy load on the exchange's service. If capacity is exceeded, it may be difficult to place or change the orders.

Many exchanges claim to have high-performance servers and bandwidth. Yet, it's advisable to review their uptime statistics. Some exchanges offer a status page announcing down time or service interruptions.

To help you get started with researching an exchange to trade with, following is a list of some of the major exchanges by currency accepted and jurisdiction:

| Exchange | Currencies | Jurisdiction |
|---|---|---|
| **Coinbase Exchange**<br>`exchange.coinbase.com` | USD, EUR | United States, European Union |
| **Bitstamp**<br>`bitstamp.net` | USD, EUR | European Union |
| **Kraken**<br>`kraken.com` | USD,EUR,GBP | United States |
| **BTC-E**<br>`btc-e.com` | USD, RUR | Bulgaria |
| **ANXPRO**<br>`anxpro.com` | USD, EUR, GBP, CHF, CAD, JPY | Hong Kong |
| **BTC China**<br>`btcchina.com` | CNY | China |

Table 4 - Exchanges that offer Bitcoin trading in various currencies

# Trading Bitcoins on an exchange

Aside from the risks involved, trading Bitcoin can be rewarding. For our introduction into trading Bitcoins, we will setup an account with Coinbase Exchange. Coinbase is a Bitcoin wallet service. They offer the option to buy and sell bitcoin from your wallet similar to Circle. In addition, they offer a full service platform for trading Bitcoin in real time.

Coinbase, founded in 2012, is funded by top-tier investors, including the New York Stock Exchange. They have a license to operate as a money transmitter in more than 15 states in the United States. Users who are living in the US and Europe can fund their accounts with US dollars or Euros.

# Setting up an account

To start trading on Coinbase Exchange, you will need to sign up with Coinbase for the wallet and verify your account. From your account you will be able to link your bank account to transfer funds. Similar to Circle's requirements, Coinbase will prompt you for a valid identification as well as a recent photo.

Open Coinbase (`https://www.coinbase.com/`) in your browser and follow the **Sign up** links (see Figure 2.9).

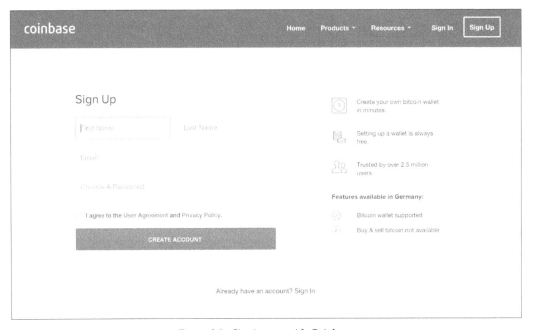

Figure 2.9 - Signing up with Coinbase

After signing up, Coinbase will ask you to verify your identity. You will be asked to verify your identity with an identification document and a recent photo.

Similar to Circle, mentioned in *Chapter 1, Setting up a Wallet*, Coinbase offers two-factor authentication. It is highly recommended to enable the two-factor authentication. If enabled, your account will be eligible for insurance in case of theft or loss.

Trading Bitcoin on Coinbase Exchange is only available to customers located in US states where Coinbase is licensed to engage in money transmission. You can find this list at

`https://www.coinbase.com/legal/licenses.`

There are other Bitcoin exchanges available where the other customers, outside of this list, can trade.

# Depositing funds

After setting up your account and verifying your identification, Coinbase will allow you to link your bank account. To add a bank account, start by logging in to your account and clicking on the **Buy/Sell Bitcoin** link on the left side navigation. From there, click on the **Payment Methods** from the links on the top navigation bar (see figure 2.10). Then click on the **+ Add a Bank Account** button. You will be prompted for your account number and details.

Simply follow the instructions provided. Coinbase will verify your account by depositing two small amounts into your bank account. When they are received, you will be asked to enter the amounts back on your account page.

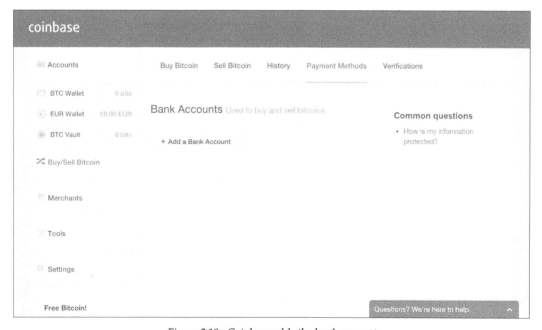

Figure 2.10 - Coinbase adds the bank account

Using your bank account, you can now deposit funds into your Coinbase USD or EUR wallet. Transfer times will vary, usually 2-5 days, depending on your bank.

 You can use Coinbase to instantly buy or sell bitcoin with funds from your bank account. The exchange rate is determined by Coinbase's pool of available bitcoin. This is different than using Coinbase Exchange. On the exchange, you buy and sell from an order book of offers placed by the other traders. The rates could vary depending on liquidity.

Once your account is setup, your identity verified, and your bank account linked, you're ready to start trading using Coinbase Exchange.

# Using Coinbase Exchange

You can access the Coinbase Exchange platform by opening `https://exchange.coinbase.com/` in your web browser. As shown next in figure 2.11, the platform offers the ability to deposit/withdraw the funds from your Coinbase wallet, has an order book for reviewing the available orders, and provides a real-time candlestick chart to support your trading activity. We will be exploring Bitcoin trading using these simple tools.

Figure 2.11 - Coinbase Exchange platform

# Funding and orders

On the left side of the screen you can find your available balance. Initially it will be zero but you can easily transfer funds from your Coinbase wallets. Transfers can be made in US dollars or in Bitcoin and are available immediately.

Underneath your available balance, you can enter Buy or Sell orders that will be posted immediately to the order book. All the orders are listed, with their price and quantity, in BTC. Your open orders are listed under the **Open Orders** section found on the lower right. From there you can cancel the existing orders. Clicking on the **Fills** link will display your completed orders.

# Order book and history

The section just to the right of your available balance is the order book. All the open orders are listed with the quantity and ordered by price. These are the orders that you can buy/sell immediately at the price listed.

In between the lowest priced sell order and the highest priced buy order is the **spread**. The spread price is an indicator of the liquidity of the market. The closer the spread price is to zero, the lower the transaction costs.

By clicking on the **Trade history** link, you can view all the orders completed from the order book.

# Price charts

On the top right you can find the price chart displayed as a candlestick chart. Each candlestick represents a fixed unit of time that can be selected from the links along the top. Moving your mouse cursor over the chart will highlight a specific point on the chart, giving you the exact price for open/close/high/low and the number of bitcoin traded, or volume.

Overlaid onto the chart is the moving average, shown as a blue and orange line. Along the bottom of the chart, you can find a bar chart showing the total number of bitcoin exchanged.

By clicking on the **Depth chart** link, you can get a view of the order book, showing how all the orders stack up, and the total price you would have to pay to buy/sell a specific number of Bitcoin. You can move your mouse cursor over the chart to see a specific price point and quantity.

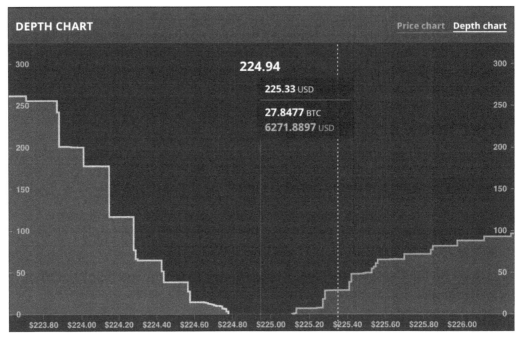

Figure 2.12 - The Depth chart

# Physical Bitcoins

So far we've been discussing about buying and selling bitcoins that are stored electronically in your wallet. They are secured by a digital private key which is encrypted by wallet software. Being completely digital, these coins are only available and managed online.

Physical Bitcoins is a concept that allows us to hold a bitcoin in our hand by embedding the private key into a precious object. The objects openly display the public address that can be used to verify that the funds are in fact available. This makes it convenient to exchange Bitcoin, hand to hand, by not having to involve a software wallet. In addition, since the private key is never stored online, it makes hacking very difficult.

As a collector's item, physical Bitcoins often have a numismatic value placed above the actual value of the electronic Bitcoin. In addition, the physical object is often a precious metal, such as gold or silver. The combined values of all these aspects are used in estimating the full value of a physical Bitcoin. You can always check marketplaces, such as eBay, to help price this value.

Before buying any physical bitcoins, make sure to do some background checks on the seller and the manufacturer of the object. They often provide information on how to ensure the validity of the item. Because the private key is often hidden, it's important to be able to verify that it hasn't been compromised.

Manufacturers have used tamper-evident holograms to protect the key. The hologram can show if there was an attempt to uncover the key. The public key can be used to check if the bitcoin has been spent. Make sure to check these two components before buying a physical bitcoin.

The following table lists some of the popular manufacturers of physical bitcoins, and information about their products:

| Manufacturer | Description |
| --- | --- |
| **Casascius**<br><br>casascius.com | One of the first manufacturers of physical bitcoin. Offers units consisting of solid brass coins, silver coins, and gold-plated bars. The private key is embedded under a card and protected by a tamper-evident hologram. |
| **Alitin Mint**<br><br>alitinmint.com | Offers coins made of pure silver. The private key is engraved around the edge of the coin and is protected by a tamper-resistant case. |
| **Titan Bitcoin**<br><br>titanbtc.com | Offers coins minted in gold and silver with the private key protected by tamper-evident hologram. |

Table 5 - Manufacturers of Physical bitcoins

# Summary

In this chapter, we briefly discussed about Bitcoin trading. We covered what can move a Bitcoin's price and the various tools to follow the changes. Following that, we introduced Bitcoin exchanges, understood how to choose one, and looked into how they worked. Finally, we ended the chapter with getting to know another way to hold bitcoins, physically in our hands.

As we saw, there are various ways to buy and sell Bitcoin as a digital currency. In all cases, the bitcoins are controlled and owned through their private key.

In the next chapter, we're going to discuss how you can protect your bitcoins by learning how to safeguard the private keys.

# 3
# Protecting Your Bitcoins

*"The governments of the world have spent hundreds and hundreds of trillions of dollars bailing out a decaying, dickensian, outmoded system called banking, when the solution to the future of finance is peer-to-peer. It's going to be alternative currencies like bitcoin and it's not actually going to be a banking system as we had before 2008."*

*– Patrick Young - financial analyst*

Up to this point, we have explored various ways to buy and sell bitcoin using an online exchange and wallet. Online wallets offer an easy-to-use system for storing bitcoins. However, the real purpose of Bitcoin is to ensure an individual's ability to store and protect his/her own money.

In this chapter, we will explore ways to safely hold your own bitcoin. We will cover the following topics:

- Storing your bitcoins
- Working with brainwallet
- Understanding deterministic wallets
- Storing Bitcoins in cold storage
- Good housekeeping with Bitcoin

# Storing your bitcoins

The banking system has a legacy of offering various financial services to its customers. They offer convenient ways to spend money, such as cheques and credit cards, but the storage of money is their base service.

For many centuries, banks have been a safe place to keep money. Customers rely on the interest paid on their deposits, as well as on the government insurance against theft and insolvency. Savings accounts have helped make preserving the wealth easy, and accessible to a large population in the western world.

Yet, some people still save a portion of their wealth as cash or precious metals, usually in a personal safe at home or in a safety deposit box. They may be those who have, over the years, experienced or witnessed the downsides of banking: government confiscation, out of control inflation, or *runs on the bank*.

Furthermore, a large population of the world does not have access to the western banking system. For those who live in remote areas or for those without credit, opening a bank account is virtually impossible. They must handle their own money properly to prevent loss or theft. In some places of the world, there can be great risk involved. These groups of people, who have little or no access to banking, are called the "underbanked".

For the underbanked population, Bitcoin offers immediate access to a global financial system. Anyone with access to the internet or who carries a mobile phone with the ability to send and receive SMS messages, can hold his or her own bitcoin and make global payments. They can essentially become their own bank.

However, you must understand that Bitcoin is still in its infancy as a technology. Similar to the Internet of circa 1995, it has demonstrated enormous potential, yet lacks usability for a mainstream audience. As a parallel, e-mail in its early days was a challenge for most users to set up and use, yet today it's as simple as entering your e-mail address and password on your smartphone. Bitcoin has yet to develop through these stages.

Yet, with some simple guidance, we can already start realizing its potential. Let's discuss some general guidelines for understanding *how to become your own bank*.

# Bitcoin savings

In most normal cases, we only keep a small amount of cash in our hand wallets to protect ourselves from theft or accidental loss. Much of our money is kept in checking or savings accounts with easy access to pay our bills. Checking accounts are used to cover our rent, utility bills, and other payments, while our savings accounts hold money for longer-term goals, such as a down payment on buying a house.

It's highly advisable to develop a similar system for managing your Bitcoin money. Both local and online wallets provide a convenient way to access your bitcoins for day-to-day transactions. Yet there is the unlikely risk that one could lose his or her Bitcoin wallet due to an accidental computer crash or faulty backup. With online wallets, we run the risk of the website or the company becoming insolvent, or falling victim to cybercrime.

By developing a reliable system, we can adopt our own personal 'Bitcoin Savings' account to hold our funds for long-term storage. Usually, these savings are kept offline to protect them from any kind of computer hacking.

With protected access to our offline storage, we can periodically transfer money to and from our savings. Thus, we can arrange our Bitcoin funds much as we manage our money with our hand wallets and checking/savings accounts.

# Paper wallets

In *Chapter 1*, *Setting up a Wallet*, we discussed public addresses and private keys. As explained, a private key is a large random number that acts as the key to spend your bitcoins. A cryptographic algorithm is used to generate a private key and, from it, a public address. We can share the public address to receive bitcoins, and, with the private key, spend the funds sent to the address.

Generally, we rely on our Bitcoin wallet software to handle the creation and management of our private keys and public addresses. As these keys are stored on our computers and networks, they are vulnerable to hacking, hardware failures, and accidental loss.

Private keys and public addresses are, in fact, just strings of letters and numbers. This format makes it easy to move the keys offline for physical storage. Keys printed on paper are called "paper wallet" and are highly portable and convenient to store in a physical safe or a bank safety deposit box. With the private key generated and stored offline, we can safely send bitcoin to its public address.

A paper wallet must include at least one private key and its computed public address. Additionally, the paper wallet can include a QR code to make it convenient to retrieve the key and address. Figure 3.1 is an example of a paper wallet generated by Coinbase:

Figure 3.1 - Paper wallet generated from Coinbase

The paper wallet includes both the public address (labeled *Public key*) and the private key, both with QR codes to easily transfer them back to your online wallet. Also included on the paper wallet is a place for notes.

This type of wallet is easy to print for safe storage. It is recommended that copies are stored securely in multiple locations in case the paper is destroyed. As the private key is shown in plain text, anyone who has access to this wallet has access to the funds.

Do not store your paper wallet on your computer. Loss of the paper wallet due to hardware failure, hacking, spyware, or accidental loss can result in complete loss of your bitcoin. *Make sure you have multiple copies of your wallet printed and securely stored before transferring your money.*

## One time use paper wallets

Transactions from bitcoin addresses must include the full amount. As described in *Chapter 1, Setting up a Wallet*, each transaction must account for the full balance of the address. When sending a partial amount to a recipient, the remaining balance must be sent to a *change address*.

Paper wallet that includes only one private key are considered to be "one time use" paper wallet. While you can always send multiple transfers of bitcoin to the wallet, it is highly recommended that you spend the coins only once. Therefore, you shouldn't move a large number of bitcoins to the wallet expecting to spend a partial amount.

With this in mind, when using one-time use paper wallet, it's recommended that you only save a usable amount to each wallet. This amount could be a block of coins that you'd like to fully redeem to your online wallet.

# Creating a paper wallet

In *Chapter 2*, *Buying and Selling Bitcoins*, we introduced an online wallet service called Coinbase. Coinbase offers an easy-to-use feature for creating paper wallets.

To create a paper wallet in Coinbase, simply log in with your username and password. Click on the **Tools** link on the left-hand side menu. Next, click on the **Paper Wallets** link from the above menu. Coinbase will prompt you to **Generate a paper wallet** and **Import a paper wallet**. Follow the links to generate a paper wallet. You can expect to see the paper wallet rendered, as shown in the following figure 3.2:

Figure 3.2 - Creating a paper wallet with Coinbase

Coinbase generates your paper wallet completely from your browser, without sending the private key back to its server. This is important to protect your private key from exposure to the network.

 You are generating the only copy of your private key. Make sure that you print and securely store multiple copies of your paper wallet before transferring any money to it. *Loss of your wallet and private key will result in the loss of your bitcoin.*

By clicking the **Regenerate** button, you can generate multiple paper wallets and store various amounts of bitcoin on each wallet. Each wallet is easily redeemable in full at Coinbase or with other bitcoin wallet services.

## Verifying your wallet's balance

After generating and printing multiple copies of your paper wallet, you're ready to transfer your funds. Coinbase will prompt you with an easy option to transfer the funds from your Coinbase wallet to your paper wallet:

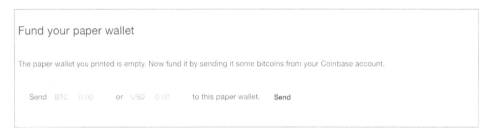

Figure 3.3 - Transferring funds to your paper wallet

Figure 3.3 shows Coinbase's prompt to transfer your funds. It provides options to enter your amount in BTC or USD. Simply specify your amount and click **Send**. Note that Coinbase only keeps a copy of your public address. You can continue to send additional amounts to your paper wallet using the same public address.

 For your first time working with paper wallets, it's advisable that you only send small amounts of bitcoin, to learn and experiment with the process. Once you feel comfortable with creating and redeeming paper wallets, you can feel secure with transferring larger amounts.

To verify that the funds have been moved to your paper wallet, we can use a blockchain explorer to verify that the funds have been confirmed by the network. Blockchain explorers make all the transaction data from the Bitcoin network available for public review.

We'll use a service called `Blockchain.info` to verify our paper wallet. Simply open `www.blockchain.info` in your browser and enter the public key from your paper wallet in the search box. If found, `Blockchain.info` will display a list of the transaction activities on that address:

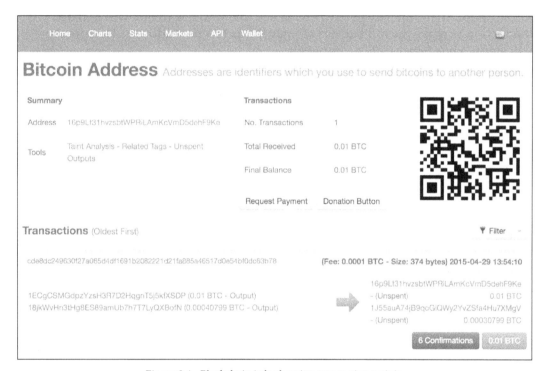

Figure 3.4 - Blockchain.info showing transaction activity

Shown in figure 3.4 is the transaction activity for the address starting with `16p9Lt`. You can quickly see the total bitcoin received and the current balance.

Under the **Transactions** section, you can find the details of the transactions recorded by the network. Also listed are the public addresses that were combined by the wallet software, as well as the change address used to complete the transfer.

 Note that at least six confirmations are required before the transaction is considered *confirmed*.

# Importing versus sweeping

When importing your private key, the wallet software will simply add the key to its list of private keys. As previously mentioned in *Chapter 1, Setting up a Wallet*, your bitcoin wallet will manage your list of private keys. When sending money, it will combine the balances from multiple addresses to make the transfer. Any remaining amount will be sent back to the change address. The wallet software will automatically manage your change addresses.

Some Bitcoin wallets offer the ability to **sweep** your private key. This involves a second step. After importing your private key, the wallet software will make a transaction to move the full balance of your funds to a new address. This process will empty your paper wallet completely.

The step to transfer the funds may require additional time to allow the network to confirm your transaction. This process could take up to one hour. In addition to the confirmation time, a small miner's fee may be applied. This fee could be in the amount of 0.0001BTC.

 If you are certain that you are the only one with access to the private key, it is safe to use the import feature. However, if you believe someone else may have access to the private key, sweeping is highly recommended.

Listed in the following table are some common bitcoin wallets which support importing a private key:

| Bitcoin Wallet | Comments | Sweeping |
|---|---|---|
| **Coinbase** <br> `https://www.coinbase.com/` | This provides direct integration between your online wallet and your paper wallet. | No |
| **Electrum** <br> `https://electrum.org` | This provides the ability to import and see your private key for easy access to your wallet's funds. | Yes |
| **Armory** <br> `https://bitcoinarmory.com/` | This provides the ability to import your private key or "sweep" the entire balance. | Yes |
| **Multibit** <br> `https://multibit.org/` | This directly imports your private key. It may use a built-in address generator for change addresses. | No |

Table 1 - Wallets that support importing private keys

# Importing your paper wallet

To import your wallet, simply log into your Coinbase account. Click on **Tools** from the left-hand side menu, followed by **Paper Wallet** from the top menu. Then, click on the **Import a paper wallet** button. You will be prompted to enter the private key of your paper wallet, as show in figure 3.5:

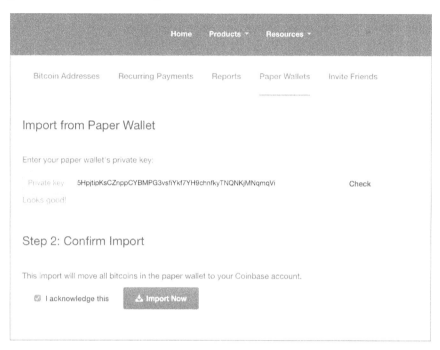

Figure 3.5 - Coinbase importing from a paper wallet

Simply enter the private key from your paper wallet. Coinbase will validate the key and ask you to confirm your import. If accepted, Coinbase will import your key and sweep your balance. The full amount will be transferred to your bitcoin wallet and become available after six confirmations.

# Paper wallet guidelines

Paper wallets display your public and private keys in plain text. Make sure that you keep these documents secure. While you can send funds to your wallet multiple times, it is highly recommended that you spend your balance only once and in full.

Before sending large amounts of bitcoin to a paper wallet, make sure you are able to test your ability to generate and import the paper wallet with small amounts of bitcoin. When you're comfortable with the process, you can rely on them for larger amounts.

As paper is easily destroyed or ruined, make sure that you keep multiple copies of your paper wallet in different locations. Make sure the location is secure from unwanted access.

Be careful with online wallet generators. A malicious site operator can obtain the private key from your web browser. Only use trusted paper wallet generators.

You can test the online paper wallet generator by opening the page in your browser while online, and then disconnecting your computer from the network. You should be able to generate your paper wallet when completely disconnected from the network, ensuring that your private keys are never sent back to the network.

Coinbase is an exception in the fact that it only sends the public address back to the server for reference. This public address is saved to make it easy to transfer funds to your paper wallet. *The private key is never saved by Coinbase when generating a paper wallet.*

## Paper wallet services

In addition to the services mentioned, there are other services that make paper wallets easy to generate and print. Listed next in Table 2 are just a few:

| Service | Notes |
|---|---|
| **BitAddress**<br>`bitaddress.org` | This offers the ability to generate single wallets, bulk wallets, brainwallets, and more. |
| **Bitcoin Paper Wallet**<br>`bitcoinpaperwallet.com` | This offers nice, stylish design, and easy-to-use features. Users can purchase holographic stickers securing the paper wallets. |
| **Wallet Generator**<br>`walletgenerator.net` | This offers printable paper wallets that fold nicely to conceal the private keys. |

Table 2 - Services for generating paper wallets and brainwallets

# Brainwallets

Storing our private keys offline by using a paper wallet is one way we can protect our coins from attacks on the network. Yet, having a physical copy of our keys is similar to holding a gold bar: it's still vulnerable to theft if the attacker can physically obtain the wallet.

One way to protect bitcoins from online or offline theft is to have the codes recallable by memory. As holding long random private keys in memory is quite difficult, even for the best of minds, we'll have to use another method to generate our private keys.

## Creating a brainwallet

Brainwallet is a way to create one or more private keys from a long phrase of random words. From the phrase, called a **passphrase**, we're able to generate a private key, along with its public addresses, to store bitcoin.

We can create any passphrase we'd like. The longer the phrase and the more random the characters, the more secure it will be.

Brainwallet phrases should contain at least 12 words. It is very important that the phrase should never come from anything published, such as a book or a song. Hackers actively search for possible brainwallets by performing brute force attacks on commonly-published phrases.

Here is an example of a brainwallet passphrase:

```
gently continue prepare history bowl shy dog accident forgive
strain dirt consume
```

Note that the phrase is composed of 12 seemingly random words. One could use an easy-to-remember sentence rather than 12 words. It's not recommended that you use a phrase from a book as hackers are continuously searching phrases from well-known sources, looking for possible brainwallets.

Regardless of whether you record your passphrase on paper or memorize it, the idea is to use a passphrase that's easy to recall and type, yet difficult to crack.

**Don't let this happen to you:**

"Just lost 4 BTC out of a hacked brain wallet. The pass phrase was a line from an obscure poem in Afrikaans. Somebody out there has a really comprehensive dictionary attack program running."

Reddit Thread (`http://redd.it/1ptuf3`)

 Unfortunately, this user lost their bitcoin because they chose a published line from a poem. *Make sure that you choose a passphrase that is composed of multiple components of non-published text.*

Sadly, although warned, some users may resort to simple phrases that are easy to crack. Simple passwords such as `123456`, `password1`, and `iloveyou` are still commonly used with e-mails, and login accounts are routinely cracked.

*Do not use simple passwords for your brainwallet passphrase. Make sure that you use at least 12 words with additional characters and numbers.*

Using the preceding paraphrase, we can generate our private key and public address using the many tools available online.

We'll use an online service called **BitAddress** to generate the actual brainwallet from the passphrase.

Simply open `www.bitaddress.org` in your browser. At first, BitAddress will ask you to move your mouse cursor around to collect enough random points to generate a seed for generating random numbers. This process could take a minute or two.

Once opened, select the option **Brain Wallet** from the top menu. In the form presented, enter the passphrase and then enter it again to confirm. Click on **View** to see your private key and public address. For the example shown in figure 3.6, we'll use the preceding passphrase example:

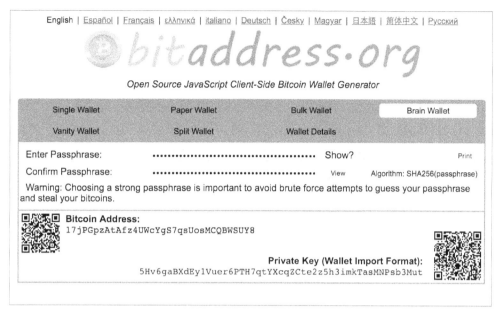

Figure 3.6 - BitAddress's brainwallet feature

From the page, you can easily copy and paste the public address and use it for receiving Bitcoin.

Later, when you're ready to spend the coins, enter the same exact passphrase to generate the same private key and public address. Referring to our Coinbase example from earlier in the chapter, we can then import the private key into our wallet.

# Increasing brainwallet security

As an early attempt to give people a way to "memorize" their Bitcoin wallet, brainwallets have become a target for hackers. Some users have chosen phrases or sentences from common books as their brainwallet. Unfortunately, the hackers who had access to large amounts of computing power were able to search for these phrases and were able to crack some brainwallets.

To improve the security of brainwallets, other methods have been developed which make brainwallets more secure. One service, called `brainwallet.io`, executes a time-intensive cryptographic function over the brainwallet phrase to create a seed that is very difficult to crack.

 It's important to know that the phase phrases used with BitAddress are not compatible with brainwallet.io.

To use brainwallet.io to generate a more secure brainwallet, open `http://brainwallet.io`:

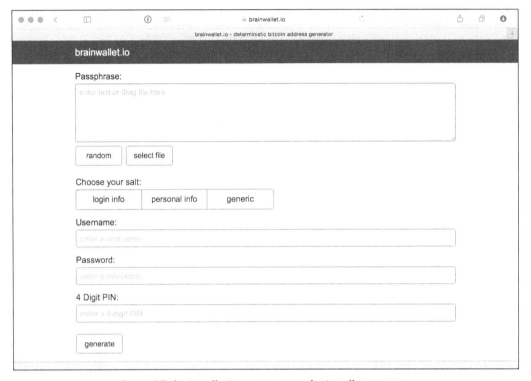

Figure 3.7 - brainwallet.io, a more secure brainwallet generator

Brainwallet.io needs a sufficient amount of entropy to generate a private key which is difficult to reproduce. Entropy, in computer science, can describe data in terms of its predictability. When data has high entropy, it could mean that it's difficult to reproduce from known sources. When generating private keys, it's very important to use data that has high entropy.

For generating brainwallet keys, we need data with high entropy, yet it should be easy for us to duplicate. To meet this requirement, brainwallet.io accepts your random passphrase, or can generate one from a list of random words. Additionally, it can use data from a file of your choice. Either way, the more entropy given, the stronger your passphrase will be. If you specify a passphrase, choosing at least 12 words is recommended.

Next, brainwallet.io prompts you for *salt*, available in several forms: login info, personal info, or generic. Salts are used to add additional entropy to the generation of your private key. Their purpose is to prevent standard dictionary attacks against your passphrase. While using brainwallet.io, this information is never sent to the server.

When ready, click the **generate** button, and the page will begin computing a **scrypt** function over your passphrase. Scrypt is a cryptographic function that requires computing time to execute. Due to the time required for each pass, it makes brute force attacks very difficult. brainwallet.io makes many thousands of passes to ensure that a strong seed is generated for the private key. Scrypt is discussed later in the book.

Once finished, your new private key and public address, along with their QR codes, will be displayed for easy printing.

As an alternative, WarpWallet is also available at `https://keybase.io/warp`. WarpWallet also computes a private key based on many thousands of scrypt passes over a passphrase and salt combination.

[  Remember that brainwallet.io passphrases are not compatible with WarpWallet passphrases. ]

# Deterministic wallets

We have introduced brainwallets that yield one private key and public address. They are designed for one time use and are practical for holding a fixed amount of bitcoin for a period of time.

Yet, if we're making lots of transactions, it would be convenient to have the ability to generate unlimited public addresses so that we can use them to receive bitcoin from different transactions or to generate change addresses.

A *Type 1 Deterministic Wallet* is a simple wallet schema based on a passphrase with an index appended. By incrementing the index, an unlimited number of addresses can be created. Each new address is indexed so that its private key can be quickly retrieved.

## Creating a deterministic wallet

To create a deterministic wallet, simply choose a strong passphrase, as previously described, and then append a number to represent an individual private key and public address.

It's practical to do this with a spreadsheet so that you can keep a list of public addresses on file. Then, when you want to spend the bitcoin, you simply regenerate the private key using the index. Let's walk through an example.

First, we choose the passphrase:

```
"dress retreat save scratch decide simple army piece scent ocean
hand become"
```

Then, we append an index, sequential number, to the passphrase:

```
"dress retreat save scratch decide simple army piece scent ocean
hand become0"
"dress retreat save scratch decide simple army piece scent ocean
hand become1"
"dress retreat save scratch decide simple army piece scent ocean
hand become2"
"dress retreat save scratch decide simple army piece scent ocean
hand become3"
"dress retreat save scratch decide simple army piece scent ocean
hand become4"
```

Then, we take each passphrase, with the corresponding index, and run it through brainwallet.io, or any other brainwallet service, to generate the public address. Using a table or a spreadsheet, we can pre-generate a list of public addresses to receive bitcoin. Additionally, we can add a balance column to help track our money:

| Index | Public Address | Balance |
|-------|----------------|---------|
| 0 | 1Bc2WZ2tiodYwYZCXRRrvzivKmrGKg2Ub9 | 0.00 |
| 1 | 1PXRtWnNYTXKQqgcxPDpXEvEDpkPKvKB82 | 0.00 |
| 2 | 1KdRGNADn7ipGdKb8VNcsk4exrHZZ7FuF2 | 0.00 |
| 3 | 1DNfd491t3ABLzFkYNRv8BWh8suJC9k6n2 | 0.00 |
| 4 | 17pZHju3KL4vVd2KRDDcoRdCs2RjyahXwt | 0.00 |

Table 3 - Using a spreadsheet to track deterministic wallet addresses

## Spending from a deterministic wallet

When we have money available in our wallet to spend, we can simply regenerate the private key for the index matching the public address.

For example, let's say we have received 2BTC on the address starting with `1KdRGN` in the preceding table. Since we know it belongs to index #2, we can reopen the brainwallet from the passphrase:

```
"dress retreat save scratch decide simple army piece scent ocean
hand become2"
```

Using brainwallet.io as our brainwallet service, we quickly regenerate the original private key and public address:

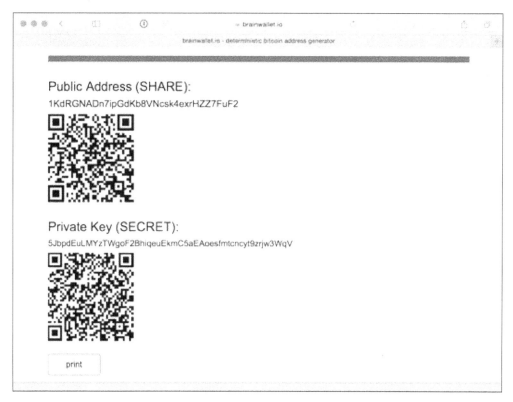

Figure 3.8 - Private key re-generated from a deterministic wallet

Finally, we import the private key into our Bitcoin wallet, as described earlier in the chapter. If we don't want to keep the change in our online wallet, we can simply send the change back to the next available public address in our deterministic wallet.

Pre-generating public addresses with deterministic wallets can be useful in many situations. Perhaps you want to do business with a partner and want to receive 12 payments over the course of one year. You can simply regenerate the 12 addresses and keep track of each payment using a spreadsheet.

Another example could apply to an e-commerce site. If you'd like to receive payment for the goods or services being sold, you can pre-generate a long list of addresses. Only storing the public addresses on your website protects you from malicious attack on your web server.

While Type 1 deterministic wallets are very useful, we'll introduce a more advanced version called the *Type 2 Hierarchical Deterministic Wallet* next.

# Type 2 Hierarchical Deterministic wallets

Type 2 Hierarchical Deterministic (HD) wallets function similarly to Type 1 deterministic wallets, as they are able to generate an unlimited amount of private keys from a single passphrase, but they offer more advanced features. HD wallets are used by desktop, mobile, and hardware wallets as a way of securing an unlimited number of keys by a single passphrase.

HD wallets are secured by a root seed. The root seed, generated from entropy, can be a number up to 64 bytes long. To make the root seed easier to save and recover, a phrase consisting of a list of mnemonic code words is rendered. The following is an example of a root seed:

```
01bd4085622ab35e0cd934adbdcce6ca
```

To render the mnemonic code words, the root seed number plus its checksum is combined and then divided into groups of 11 bits. Each group of bits represents an index between 0 and 2047. The index is then mapped to a list of 2,048 words. For each group of bits, one word is listed, as shown in the following example, which generates the following phrase:

```
essence forehead possess embarrass giggle spirit further
understand fade appreciate angel suffocate
```

 BIP-0039 details the specifications for creating mnemonic code words to generate a deterministic key, and is available at https://en.bitcoin. it/wiki/BIP_0039.

In the HD wallet, the root seed is used to generate a master private key and a master chain code. The master private key is used to generate a master public key, as with normal Bitcoin private keys and public keys.

These keys are then used to generate additional children keys in a tree-like structure. Figure 3.9 illustrates the process of creating the master keys and chain code from a root seed:

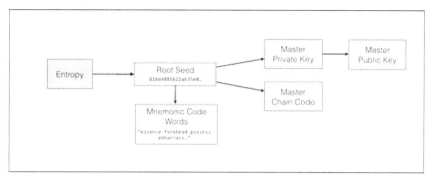

Figure 3.9 - Generating an HD Wallet's root seed, code words, and master keys

Using a *child key derivation* function, children keys can be generated from the master or parent keys. An index is then combined with the keys and the chain code to generate and organize parent/child relationships. From each parent, two billion children keys can be created, and from each child's private key, the public key and public address can be created.

In addition to generating a private key and a public address, each child can be used as a parent to generate its own list of child keys. This allows the organization of the derived keys in a tree-like structure. Hierarchically, an unlimited amount of keys can be created in this way.

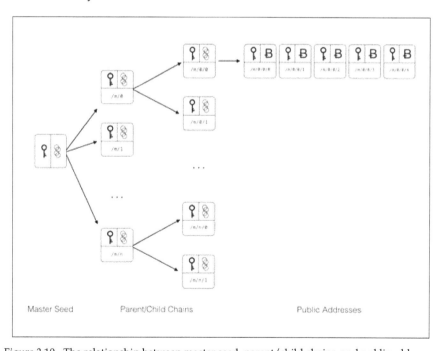

Figure 3.10 - The relationship between master seed, parent/child chains, and public addresses

HD wallets are very practical as thousands of keys and public addresses can be managed by one seed. The entire tree of keys can be backed up and restored simply by the passphrase.

HD wallets can be organized and shared in various useful ways. For example, in a company or organization, a parent key and chain code could be issued to generate a list of keys for each department. Each department would then have the ability to render its own set of private/public keys.

Alternatively, a public parent key can be given to generate child public keys, but not the private keys. This can be useful in the example of an audit. The organization may want the auditor to perform a balance sheet on a set of public keys, but without access to the private keys for spending.

Another use case for generating public keys from a parent public key is for e-commerce. As an example mentioned previously, you may have a website and would like to generate an unlimited amount of public addresses. By generating a public parent key for the website, the shopping card can create new public addresses in real time.

HD wallets are very useful for Bitcoin wallet applications. Next, we'll look at a software package called **Electrum** for setting up an HD wallet to protect your bitcoins.

# Installing a HD wallet

HD wallets are very convenient and practical. To show how we can manage an unlimited number of addresses by a single passphrase, we'll install an HD wallet software package called Electrum.

Electrum is an easy-to-use desktop wallet that runs on Windows, OS/X, and Linux. It implements a secure HD wallet that is protected by a 12-word passphrase. It is able to synchronize with the blockchain, using servers that index all the Bitcoin transactions, to provide quick updates to your balances.

Electrum has some nice features to help protect your bitcoins. It supports multi-signature transactions, that is transactions that require more than one key to spend coins. Multi-signature transactions are useful when you want to share the responsibility of a Bitcoin address between two or more parties, or to add an extra layer of protection to your Bitcoins.

Additionally, Electrum has the ability to create a *watching-only* version of your wallet. This allows you to give access to your public keys to another party without releasing the private keys. This can be very useful for auditing or accounting purposes.

To install Electrum, simply open the URL `https://electrum.org/#download` and follow the instructions for your operating system. On first installation, Electrum will create for you a new wallet identified by a passphrase. Make sure that you protect this passphrase offline!

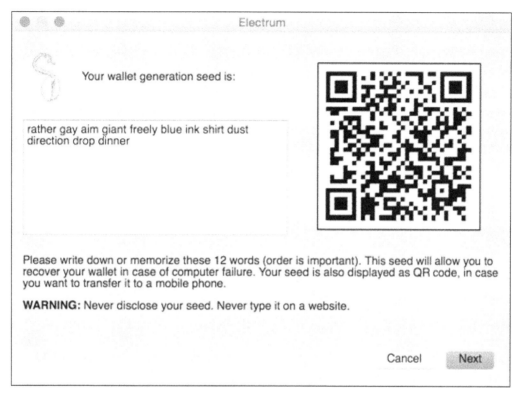

Figure 3.11 - Recording the passphrase from an Electrum wallet

Electrum will proceed by asking you to re-enter the passphrase to confirm you have it recorded. Finally, it will ask you for a password. This password is used to encrypt your wallet's seed and any private keys imported into your wallet on-disk. You will need this password any time you send bitcoins from your account.

# Bitcoins in cold storage

If you are responsible for a large amount of bitcoin which can be exposed to online hacking or hardware failure, it is important to minimize your risk. A common schema for minimizing the risk is to split your online wallet between *Hot wallet* and *Cold Storage*.

A hot wallet refers to your online wallet used for everyday deposits and withdrawals. Based on your customers' needs, you can store the minimum needed to cover the daily business. For example, Coinbase claims to hold approximately five percent of the total bitcoins on deposit in their hot wallet. The remaining amount is stored in cold storage.

Cold storage is an offline wallet for bitcoin. Addresses are generated, typically from a deterministic wallet, with their passphrase and private keys stored offline. Periodically, depending on their day-to-day needs, bitcoins are transferred to and from the cold storage.

Additionally, bitcoins may be moved to **Deep cold storage**. These bitcoins are generally more difficult to retrieve. While cold storage transfer may easily be done to cover the needs of the hot wallet, a deep cold storage schema may involve physically accessing the passphrase / private keys from a safe, a safety deposit box, or a bank vault. The reasoning is to slow down the access as much as possible.

# Cold storage with Electrum

We can use Electrum to create a hot wallet and a cold storage wallet. To exemplify, let's imagine a business owner who wants to accept bitcoin from his PC cash register. For security reasons, he may want to allow access to the generation of new addresses to receive Bitcoin, but not access to spending them. Spending bitcoins from this wallet will be secured by a protected computer.

To start, create a normal Electrum wallet on the protected computer. Secure the passphrase and assign a strong password to the wallet. Then, from the menu, select **Wallet | Master Public Keys**. The key will be displayed as shown in figure 3.12. Copy this number and save it to a USB key.

Figure 3.12 - Your Electrum wallet's public master key

Your master public key can be used to generate new public keys, but without access to the private keys. As mentioned in the previous examples, this has many practical uses, as in our example with the cash register.

Next, from your cash register, install Electrum. On setup, or from **File | New/Restore**, choose **Restore a wallet or import keys** and the **Standard wallet** type:

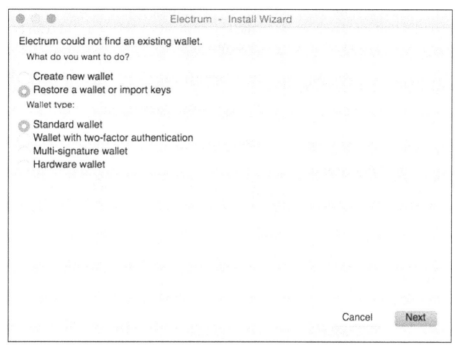

Figure 3.13 - Setting up a cash register wallet with Electrum

On the next screen, Electrum will prompt you to enter your public master key. Once accepted, Electrum will generate your wallet from the public master key. When ready, your new wallet will be ready to accept bitcoin without access to the private keys.

**WARNING:**

If you import private keys into your Electrum wallet, they cannot be restored from your passphrase or public master key. They have not been generated by the root seed and exist independently in the wallet.

If you import private keys, make sure to back up the wallet file after every import.

# Verifying access to a private key

When working with public addresses, it may be important to prove that you have access to a private key. By using Bitcoin's cryptographic ability to sign a message, you can verify that you have access to the key without revealing it. This can be offered as proof from a trustee that they control the keys.

Using Electrum's built-in message signing feature, we can use the private key in our wallet to sign a message. The message, combined with the digital signature and public address, can later be used to verify that it was signed with the original private key.

To begin, choose an address from your wallet. In Electrum, your addresses can be found under the **Addresses** tab. Next, right click on an address and choose **Sign/verify Message**. A dialog box allowing you to sign a message will appear:

Figure 3.13 - Electrum's Sign/Verify Message features

As shown in figure 3.13, you can enter any message you like and sign it with the private key of the address shown. This process will produce a digital signature that can be shared with others to prove that you have access to the private key.

To verify the signature on another computer, simply open Electrum and choose **Tools | Sign | Verify** Message from the menu. You will be prompted with the same dialog as shown in figure 3.13. Copy and paste the message, the address, and the digital signature, and click **Verify**. The results will be displayed.

By requesting a signed message from someone, you can verify that they do, in fact, have control of the private key. This is useful for making sure that the trustee of a cold storage wallet has access to the private keys without releasing or sharing them.

Another good use of message signing is to prove that someone has control of some quantity of bitcoin. By signing a message that includes the public address with funds, one can see that the party is the owner of the funds.

Finally, signing and verifying a message can be useful for testing your backups. You can test that your private key and public address completely offline without actually sending bitcoin to the address.

# Good housekeeping with Bitcoin

To ensure the safe-keeping of your bitcoin, it's important to protect your private keys by following a short list of best practices:

- **Never store your private keys unencrypted on your hard drive or in the cloud**: Unencrypted wallets can easily be stolen by hackers, viruses, or malware. Make sure your keys are always encrypted before being saved to disk.

- **Never send money to a Bitcoin address without a backup of the private keys**: It's really important that you have a backup of your private key before sending money its public address. There are stories of early adopters who have lost significant amounts of bitcoin because of hardware failures or inadvertent mistakes.

- **Always test your backup process by repeating the recovery steps**: When setting up a backup plan, make sure to test your plan by backing up your keys, sending a small amount to the address, and recovering the amount from the backup. Message signing and verification is also a useful way to test your private key backups offline.

- **Ensure that you have a secure location for your paper wallets**: Unauthorized access to your paper wallets can result in the loss of your bitcoin. Make sure that you keep your wallets in a secure safe, in a bank safety deposit box, or in a vault. It's advisable to keep copies of your wallets in multiple locations.

- **Keep multiple copies of your paper wallets**: Paper can easily be damaged by water or direct sunlight. Make sure that you keep multiple copies of your paper wallets in plastic bags, protected from direct light with a cover.

- **Consider writing a testament or will for your Bitcoin wallets**: The testament should name who has access to the bitcoin and how they will be distributed. Make sure that you include instructions on how to recover the coins.

- **Never forget your wallet's password or passphrase**: This sounds obvious, but it must be emphasized. There is no way to recover a lost password or passphrase.

- **Always use a strong passphrase**: A strong passphrase should meet the following requirements:

  ° It should be long and difficult to guess

  ° It should not be from a famous publication: literature, holy books, and so on

  ° It should not contain personal information

  ° It should be easy to remember and type accurately

  ° It should not be reused between sites and applications

# Summary

So far, we've covered the basics of how to get started with Bitcoin. We've provided a tutorial for setting up an online wallet and for how to buy Bitcoin in 15 minutes. We've covered online exchanges and marketplaces, and how to safely store and protect your bitcoin.

In the next few chapters, we're going to dive deeper into Bitcoin by setting up a node, exploring how the blockchain works, and doing some actual bitcoin programming.

# 4
# Understanding the Blockchain

*"With e-currency based on cryptographic proof, without the need to trust a third party middleman, money can be secure and transactions effortless."*

*– Satoshi Nakamoto, Bitcoin developer*

Bitcoin's underlying transaction database is called the **Blockchain**. Its novel design, as a distributed ledger, allows it to function without any trusted central authority. Understanding how it works is essential for integrating information systems with Bitcoin. In this chapter, you will be given a simplified explanation of the blockchain's internal mechanisms. Building on the previous chapters, we'll cover the following subjects in more detail:

- Keys, transactions, and blocks
- Digital signatures
- Cryptographic hashes
- The Blockchain
- Nodes and miners
- Decentralized design
- Network attacks
- Alternative coins

## The Genesis block

September 15th, 2008 marked a defining moment for the finance industry, as Lehman Brothers, at that time the fourth largest investment bank, filed for chapter 11 bankruptcy after massive losses in stock price and assets. The collapse marked the beginning of the Global Financial Crisis of 2008.

Shortly after, Bitcoin, a new type of virtual currency, was launched by an anonymous developer, or group of developers, under the name Satoshi Nakamoto. The software was built on a publicly-accessible transaction ledger, that is distributed and validated by a network of independent nodes. More importantly, its design was powerfully resilient to attacks.

The mysterious developer launched Bitcoin at the beginning of 2009. Encoded in the first block of transactions was a message highly relevant to the state of global financial affairs at that time:

> *"The Times 03/Jan/2009 Chancellor on brink of second bailout for banks."*

The first block of transactions, called the "genesis block", set forth Bitcoin, a new peer-to-peer digital currency. As the quoted headline was published by The Times on January 3, 2009, the message acts as proof that the block was indeed created after that time. From the intention of the comment on the failure of fractional reserve lending, we get a glimpse into the mind of its developer, Satoshi Nakamoto.

Simply put, fractional reserve banking allows a bank to lend more money than it has on reserve. The modern financial system largely accepts the practice of fractional reserve banking with policy controlled by a central bank. The central bank's primary method of control is through interest rates.

More importantly, Bitcoin and its technology **The Blockchain** was released and open sourced to the world. The Bitcoin Blockchain was a solution to the difficult problem of preventing double spending when creating a distributed virtual currency.

**Double spending** occurs when two transactions are accepted with an amount that exceeds the available balance. Up until that time, a decentralized solution to the double spending problem remained open. Satoshi's solution was the Blockchain.

# Satoshi Nakamoto

Satoshi Nakamoto has remained anonymous since releasing Bitcoin. Records of his e-mails and forum posts exist from the end of 2008 through 2010. During that time, he worked with developers to release the source code and respond to the development topics. He also commented on relevant financial topics such as banking and fractional reserve lending.

Satoshi Nakamoto's e-mails and forum posts have been archived on the website of the Satoshi Nakamoto Institute (http://satoshi.nakamotoinstitute.org). It's a great resource for understanding the intentions behind the design of Bitcoin.

As quickly as he appeared, he vanished without much trace. To this day, we don't have much information on him. Many people have theorized about who Satoshi could be, yet nothing we have is conclusive.

However mysterious his character may be, his legacy remains the Bitcoin whitepaper.

# The whitepaper

The Bitcoin whitepaper was released to the public on October 31st, 2008, a couple of months before Bitcoin's blockchain was launched. In the whitepaper, Satoshi explained how the blockchain could support a purely decentralized e-currency without the need for a central authority. Satoshi writes:

> *A purely peer-to-peer version of electronic cash would allow online payments to be sent directly from one party to another without the burdens of going through a financial institution.*

The whitepaper mentions the issues with relying on the financial institutions as trusted third parties to process transactions. He particularly mentioned the costs of mediating reversible transactions which put merchants at risk of fraud, thus increasing transaction costs. The principal design goal was to ensure that whoever owns the keys controls the money. The common scenario involves a buyer who orders an item from a merchant using a credit card. As fraud against the merchant, the buyer can dispute the payment or claim an unauthorized payment. In Bitcoin, reversing the transaction is not possible.

Satoshi proposed a solution that relies on cryptographic proof. Transactions are signed and distributed on a public network. The design allows irreversible transactions sent directly between peers without centralized authority.

He was able to deliver the solution, based on a new type of data structure called the blockchain.

You can download a copy of the Bitcoin whitepaper from https://bitcoin.org/bitcoin.pdf.

# The blockchain

The public ledger which records each Bitcoin transaction is built on a data structure called the **blockchain**. Transactions are grouped into blocks, and shared and validated by a network of nodes. Consensus on the network determines which blocks are accepted.

Previously, the double-spending problem was difficult to solve without a trusted third party. To be able to accept a transaction, the available balance had to be validated by a central authority, ensuring synchronization between all the transactions.

Implementing this in a decentralized way was difficult because of the complexities of sharing data between independent nodes. If two transactions were created at the same time, but with only enough funds available for the first transaction, the second must be rejected: the double spending problem.

As we examine the blockchain, we will see how it solves the double spending problem in a resilient and decentralized way.

# Keys, transactions, and blocks

To help you understand how Bitcoin transactions work, we'll need to explain how some of its basic mechanisms work with various cryptographic algorithms. With the classic example of sending money between Alice and Bob, we will illustrate how the Bitcoin network confirms a transaction.

# Creating a transaction

Let's start with an example where Alice wants to send 4.0BTC to Bob. Alice has a bitcoin wallet with two addresses along with the corresponding private keys that control the two amounts 1.2BTC and 2.8BTC. To receive the money, Bob will generate a private key with a Bitcoin address:

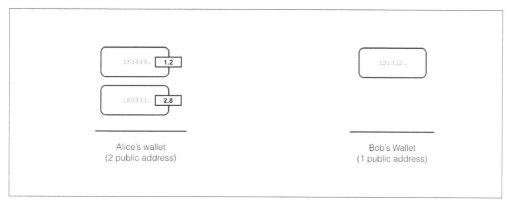

Figure 4.1 - Alice has a wallet with two addresses. Bob has a wallet with
one address. Alice wants to send 4.0BTC to Bob.

To transfer the bitcoin, we need to create a valid transaction and broadcast it to
the Bitcoin network for confirmation. If confirmed by the network, the transferred
amount will be available for spending by the receiver.

The transaction can record a transfer between two or more parties, using many
inputs for the sources of bitcoin and many outputs for the receivers of bitcoin.
Inputs and outputs are used to move the money between the addresses.

Each input must reference exactly one output from a previous transaction. Thus, on
the blockchain, bitcoin is sent through scripts which *hand-off* the money between the
addresses. As each address is controlled by a private key, the money is transferred
between the owners of the private keys. There is sometimes the misconception that
there is a *single bitcoin* that gets moved, when in fact there is no bitcoin, or fraction
of a bitcoin, that is individually assigned to an address. Transfers of bitcoins are
actually controlled by matching the inputs and outputs of the previous transactions.
Thus, the full history of transactions funding the transaction are needed to validate
a transfer.

The following Figure 4.3, illustrates how the transactions are used to connect the inputs and outputs to send bitcoin. From the example, Alice will send 4.0BTC by combining her two addresses as inputs. Written in the transaction, the amounts 1.2BTC and 2.8BTC are listed as inputs from Alice and sent to Bob as an output with the amount of 4.0BTC.

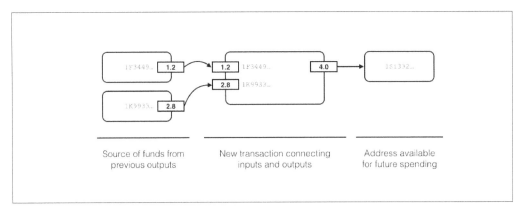

Figure 4.3 - Bitcoin transaction showing its two inputs and one output

Before broadcasting the transaction, we'll need to prove to the network that Alice was the original sender of the transaction. By proving to the network that we have the private keys, the nodes validating the transaction can agree that the transaction originated from the owner.

For each public address listed in Alice's wallet, there is a private key. With her private keys, she can sign the transaction using a *digital signature*. Verification of the signature is proof that she signed the transaction and that it hasn't been modified since.

After the transaction has been confirmed by the network, Bob will have 4.0BTC available to spend as an input to a new transaction. The linkage continues as transactions continue connecting the inputs and the outputs. Imagining the chain of transactions, one can see how quickly the money is fanned out between new addresses.

# Digital signatures

One classic problem addressed by cryptography is how one party can send a document to another party with proof that it was not modified or forged. For example, let's say Alice has a message that she wants to send to Bob. Before trusting the document, Bob wants to be sure that the message has not been modified:

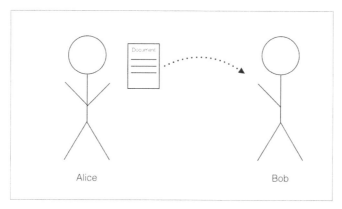

Figure 4.3 - Bob requests proof that the document originated from Alice

Alice needs a way to digitally sign the document with proof that it's an exact copy of the original document. Using a **digital signature**, Bob can verify the copy. If valid, he can be sure that the document has not been modified.

Digital signatures rely on a set of keys designated as **public** and **private**. Signing a document with a private key creates a signature that can be verified with its associated public key. Any signed document verified by the public key can be assumed to be original.

# Public key encryption

Public key encryption is a cryptographic algorithm that uses two mathematically generated keys to encrypt and decrypt a message, or to digitally sign a document. The private key is used to encrypt or sign the document, and the public key is used to decrypt the message or verify the signature.

The two keys are generated at the same time by an **asymmetric cryptographic algorithm**. The keys are mathematically bound and cannot be interchanged. In other words, the public key only functions with its corresponding private key.

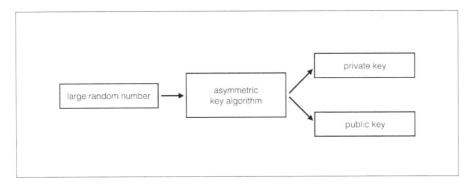

Figure 4.4 - Asymmetric key algorithms generate a public and private key from a large random number

Public and private keys are simply long numbers. An example private key looks as follows:

```
3082011302010104209ea335d666d9e097c5a5e92ef32228a18c3615aa38e13fb593712
a11f039c148a081a53081a2020101302c06072a8648ce3d0101022100ffffffffffffffff
fffffffffffffffffffffffffffffffffffffffffffeffffffc2f30060401000401070441 0479
be667ef9dcbbac55a06295ce870b07029bfcdb2dce28d959f2815b16f81798483ada7726
a3c4655da4fbfc0e1108a8fd17b448a68554199c47d08ffb10d4b8022100ffffffffffffffff
fffffffffffffffffebaaedce6af48a03bbfd25e8cd0364141020101a14403420004
a6b634eb85a8d9d6fe34bc6666760b3343c40f7709392541bc2d3b7666eda4d7c7c8dd57
8af2790870a591c0f17e285ce99cb2dd950b37b00f1031675bb678d6
```

Its public key looks as shown next:

```
04a6b634eb85a8d9d6fe34bc6666760b3343c40f7709392541bc2d3b7666eda4d7c7
c8dd578af2790870a591c0f17e285ce99cb2dd950b37b00f1031675bb678d6
```

These two keys are mathematically related and cannot be interchanged with any other key.

# Signing a document

In the example with Alice and Bob, using encryption software, Alice creates a public and private key pair. She then sends a copy of the public key to Bob. As the public key can only be generated by the private key, Bob can assume that Alice is the holder of the private key.

Before sending the document to Bob, Alice signs the document with her private key and includes the signature in the document.

Later, when Bob receives the document, he can verify the signature with the copy of the document. If the signature is valid, Bob can safely assume that Alice was the signer:

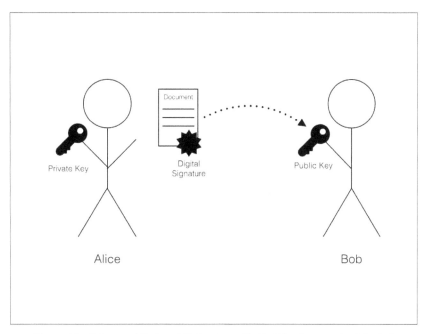

Figure 4.1 - Bob uses Alice's public key to verify that the document originated from her and has not been modified.

# Elliptic Curve Cryptography

Bitcoin uses **Elliptic Curve Digital Signature Algorithms (ECDSA)**, for generating public/private key pairs. The algorithm generates random keys based on the mathematics around elliptic curves.

Due to its features, ECDSA is suitable for signing Bitcoin transactions. For example, some algorithms can only generate both keys at the same time. With the ECDSA algorithm, a public key can be generated from a private key any time but not the other way around.

# Bitcoin addresses

Bitcoin addresses are generated from the public key through a few steps that involve **cryptographic hashes**. To explain the process, we'll first introduce cryptographic hashing algorithms.

# Cryptographic hashes

Cryptographic hashing algorithms, or just hashes, are functions that can produce a **digest** of a document. The digest is usually a small string of characters, depending on the hashing algorithm used. As one example, the popular hashing algorithm called SHA256 produces a digest 40 characters in length from a document of any size.

The smallest change to the document will produce a radically different digest. Thus, a digest can be used to verify the changes between the documents.

There is a mathematical relationship between the document and its digest, but it is impossible to generate a document from its digest. Digests do not contain enough information:

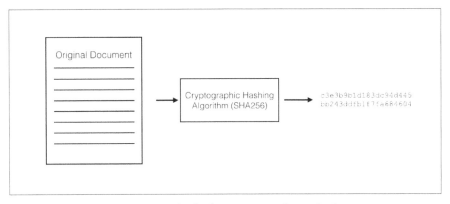

Figure 4.6 - Cryptographic hashes generate a digest of a document,
representing the document in its original state.

The digest is useful for verifying if any changes have been made between a copy and its original. By comparing the copy's hash against the original hash, we can verify if the contents have been modified. Thus, cryptographic hashes can be used to seal a valid copy (see Figure 4.7).

In Bitcoin, digital signatures are applied to the transaction and are used to verify that it was created by the holder of the private keys. The Bitcoin address that is used to send the money is created by using different hashing algorithms. The signature and Bitcoin address are both included in the transaction. If valid, the transfer of money can be confirmed on the network.

Bitcoin relies on cryptographic hashes for many of its internal functions. Primarily, every transaction is hashed and the digest is signed to ensure that no changes have been made since it was created by the sender. Blocks of transactions are also hashed to make sure no changes have been made to its list of transactions.

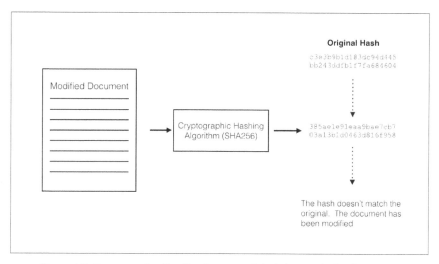

Figure 4.7 - By comparing the digests we can detect changes in the document.

# Generating a Bitcoin address

Bitcoin addresses are generated from the public key hash of an ECDSA key pair. Let's walk through a simplified explanation of this process with the follow pair:

**Private Key:**

18E14A7B6A307F426A94F8114701E7C8E774E7F9A47E2C2035DB29A206321725

**Public Key Hash:**

600FFE422B4E00731A59557A5CCA46CC183944191006324A447BDB2D98D4B408

The public/private keys listed in the chapter are given in "Hexadecimal" format. Typically, we count numbers with the digits 0 through 9. In hexadecimal, we count with the digits 0 through 9 plus A, B, C, D, E, and F. Thus, in hexadecimal format, there are 16 digits to represent a value. Counting to the decimal number 32 in hexadecimal would look as follows:

0,1,2,3,4,5,6,7,8,9,A,B,C,D,E,F,10,11,12,13,14,15,16,17,18,19,1A,1B,1C,1D,1E,1F

To generate the Bitcoin address, SHA256 and RIPEMD-160 hashing functions are first applied to the public key:

```
010966776006953D5567439E5E39F86A0D273BEE
```

To identify which network the address is intended for, a network identifier is added to the front of the address. In the preceding example, we simply add `00`, which identifies the main network, to the beginning of the key:

```
00010966776006953D5567439E5E39F86A0D273BEE
```

The main network is the official blockchain network used for public transactions. In addition to the main network, there is also a test network, named **Testnet3**, used by the developers to test bug fixes and new functionality.

Next, a checksum is calculated. Checksums are used to ensure that the address has a valid set of characters. That is, if one of the characters is mistyped, the checksum digit will be invalid. Thus, Bitcoin wallets can use the checksum to make sure you didn't enter a bogus Bitcoin address. In the previous example, the checksum is calculated as "D61967F6" and appended to the end of the string:

```
00010966776006953D5567439E5E39F86A0D273BEED61967F6
```

Finally, a `BASE58` function is applied to the network identifier, hash, and checksum. `BASE58` is a way to encode large numeric values into an alphanumeric string of characters. The `BASE58` value can be easily read or written by humans, making it practical for creating Bitcoin public addresses.

```
16UwLL9Risc3QfPqBUvKofHmBQ7wMtjvM
```

The result is a public address we can use to receive bitcoin and the private key needed to spend them. Using our Bitcoin wallet or other tools, we can generate unlimited random private keys and their addresses. This process is usually automated.

In summary, we create a private key and its Bitcoin address by starting with a large random number. An Elliptic Curve algorithm is used to generate the private/ public key pair from the random number. Finally, the Bitcoin address is generated by transforming the public key through several hashing functions, appending a checksum, and encoding it with `BASE58`.

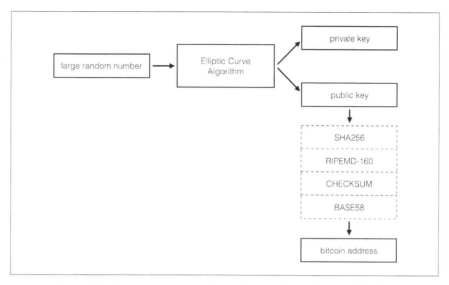

Figure 4.7 - The process of generating a Bitcoin address from a public key

# Signing a transaction

The last step needed before broadcasting the transaction to the network is to include a digital signature.

Using the private keys from each input address listed, the sender can prove that they have ownership of the funds stored in the address. The network can then verify the signature with access to the public key. Transactions with invalid digital signatures are simply discarded.

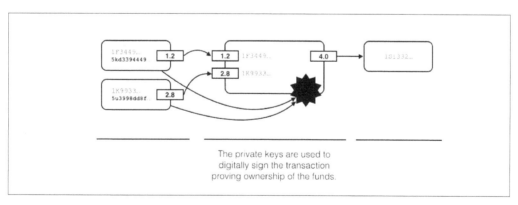

Figure 4.8 - A Bitcoin transaction with the attached digital signature.

At any point, the private key is never shared. Figure 4.8 illustrates the digital signature and how it's attached to the transaction.

Once signed, our valid transaction is now ready to broadcast to the Bitcoin network for confirmation.

# Decentralized network

The Bitcoin network consists of many thousands of nodes, with some called **miners**, and each connected directly to one another. Unlike a centralized or distributed network, Bitcoin relies on a **decentralized network**.

A decentralized network is extremely resilient because there is no central point of failure. If one or more nodes are taken offline, the remaining nodes can reroute their connection to the network through other online nodes.

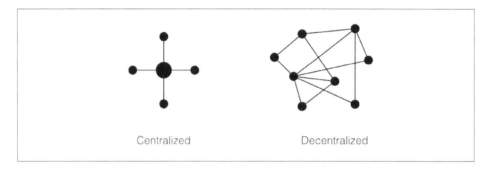

Centralized          Decentralized

Figure 4.9 - Centralized networks have a single point of failure; this is not so with decentralized networks.

In fact, the early incarnation of the Internet, called ARPANET and built by the US Department of Defense, used a decentralized design to build an information network that would be able to function even if a large portion of the network was down.

Bitcoin is a money protocol that is built on a decentralized network. Each node is independent and can join or leave the network at any time. While on the network, each node can talk to the other nodes using the Bitcoin protocol. With this protocol, it's able to script and validate the transactions or other types of digital contracts.

Bitcoin is essentially programmable money designed to run on a decentralized network.

# Broadcasting the transaction

To broadcast our signed transaction to the network, we first need to connect to one or more of the existing nodes. When connected, our node becomes part of the network and is able to send and receive transactions.

The nodes on the network listen for broadcasted transactions and share them with the other nodes. Each node can maintain a copy of every transaction created, and use them to validate new bitcoin transactions and ensure there's sufficient balance before relaying them to the other nodes.

New transactions broadcast to the network are initially labeled as *unconfirmed*, meaning that the network has not yet agreed that they are valid. A transaction must have sufficient balance and a valid digital signature before it can be validated.

Valid transactions are grouped and into a *block* by the miner. After a verification process, which involves a difficult mathematical problem, the confirmed blocks are accepted and exchanged between the nodes. The blocks of transactions are time-stamped and chained together to form a "blockchain". Each node maintains its own copy of the blockchain and repeats the process by listening for new transactions.

# The blockchain

Bitcoin uses a unique and novel way of storing and distributing its transaction ledger. To create a database of transactions that is both resilient and transparent, it distributes all its transactions across a global network of nodes. This database is called the blockchain. To understand how the blockchain works, we'll explore how the blocks are used to group and distribute the transactions.

# Blocks

The blockchain is a chain of blocks linked together, from the genesis block to the latest block, as shown in the following Figure 4.11. Every node connected to the network maintains a complete copy of the entire blockchain. This redundancy results in a very resilient system.

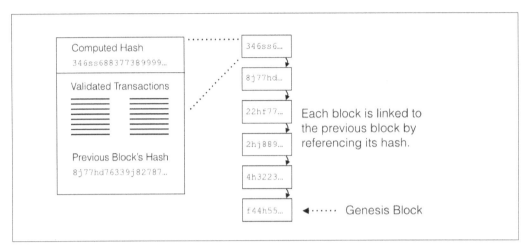

Figure 4.11 - The blockchain consists of many blocks chained together.

New blocks are mined by the **nodes** listening for transactions on the network. The nodes can share and relay the transactions amongst themselves. When a new transaction is received by a node, it is added to the new block. The new block is kept locally until a difficult computing problem is solved using the new block as the base of the solution.

New blocks with solutions to the difficult problem are eligible for a reward of newly mined bitcoin, plus the transaction fees included with each transaction.

Referring back to cryptographic hashes, a hash value is used to represent the confirmation of the block. A hash value is computed on the block and its transactions, along with the hash value of the previous block. Any changes to the block can be validated against its hash.

The chains of hashes are critical to the integrity of the chain. Each new block contains within it the hash of the previous block. If any of the transactions are modified, the hash, as well as the rest of the chain, becomes invalid. Therefore, as the chain grows and more copies of it are maintained by independent miners, the more difficult it becomes to modify the public ledger.

Today, the Bitcoin network's combined computing power is noted as the largest supercomputer on earth. The large amount of computer power is what protects the Bitcoin network from attacks. Any attacker would need to overtake more than half of the network's computer power to be able to double spend.

The result is a database of transactions that are distributed for redundancy and cryptographically protected from modifications. Anyone can download a copy of the blockchain and query it for transactions. With the full blockchain, the value of any address can be known for any point in time. The addresses with unspent balances can then be used as inputs to a new transaction.

# Forks

Due to their independent nature, the network of nodes can consist of either *honest* or *malicious* nodes. Honest nodes only accept valid transactions and reject any that double spend or have invalid signatures. Malicious nodes may make an attempt to accept a corrupt transaction or selectively reject the other transactions.

To isolate and reject the bad nodes on the network, consensus between the nodes exists on what ruleset to accept. This consensus determines which blocks are accepted on the network. Since the genesis block, a large majority of the nodes have agreed to "play nicely" rather than to corrupt, due to the reward of earning new bitcoin. This consensus forms the longest and most trustworthy chain.

Due to changes in how the nodes can accept/reject blocks, it is possible for the blockchain to *fork* and create a side blockchain. Figure 4.12 illustrates a blockchain fork:

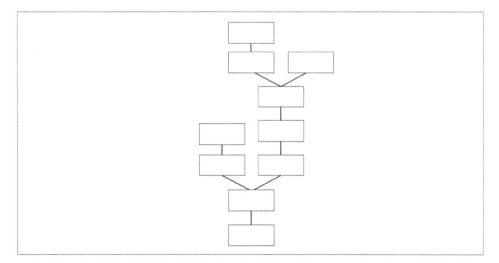

Figure 4.12 - Blockchains can fork

If a corrupted block is detected by the network, the result is a fork in the chain. Without validations from the network, the blocks become orphans and the fork invalid. Valid blocks are added to the valid portion of the chain. From the network's perspective, the longest chain of valid blocks is considered the official blockchain. From any block, there is one path back to the genesis block.

> The *longest chain* actually includes the total *difficulty* needed to produce the chain, not just the individual blocks. This is important for certain types of attacks. Difficulty and attacks will be covered later in the chapter.

Blocks from shorter chains are called *orphans*. Orphans are eventually abandoned and not used for anything. All the valid transactions included in the shorter chain are copied and added to a new block, and eventually integrated into the longer chain.

Bug fixes or major version updates can also cause a fork in the blockchain. As new nodes implement a version update, the result can be a fork and change. This is how the Bitcoin network accepts or rejects the changes to the protocol and software. Therefore, it's possible to have multiple versions of the software evolve through the blockchain.

> Back in March of 2013, a miner running version 0.8.0 of the software released a block that was incompatible with the other miners. To resolve this issue, the miners were asked to revert to 0.7.0 until a fix was issued. After the fix was released, a hard fork in the chain resulted. For the most part it was seamless. However, the miners operating on the 0.8.0 fork lost their mining rewards.

In summary, all the nodes connected to the Bitcoin network can relay transactions. The nodes are connected to each other through a decentralized network. To validate transactions, each node maintains a full copy of the blockchain. The blockchain is built from a chain of blocks. Each block contains a list of valid transactions and is linked to the previous block in the chain.

While all the nodes help to build the Bitcoin network, some nodes can choose to mine for new bitcoins. These nodes are called **Miners**. **Mining** is the process of using a new block of transactions as the base to a difficult puzzle to solve with computational power. If it is solved, the miner is rewarded new bitcoins, plus the transaction fees included with each transaction.

# The Bitcoin supply

The total number of Bitcoins is fixed at 21 million and is distributed as a reward to the miners who solve a difficult computing problem. Rewards are given out approximately every 10 minutes, depending on the total number of miners competing for the reward. The difficulty of the problem is adjusted, to compensate for the changes in the number of miners competing, every two weeks.

Starting with the genesis block in the year 2009, 50 bitcoins were released as rewards. After every 210,000 blocks, the reward is halved to compensate for the anticipated increase in global computer power. It takes about four years to mine 210,000 blocks.

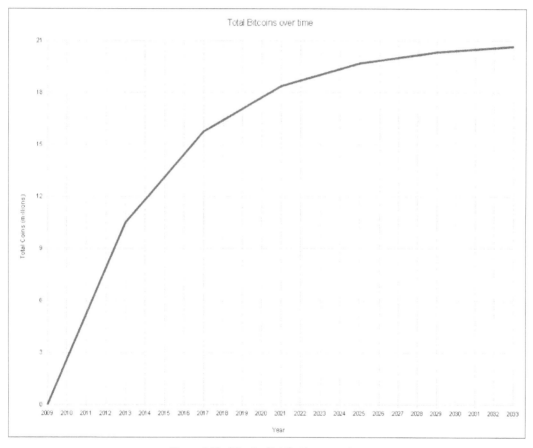

Figure 4.13 - Bitcoin distribution over time

In the preceding figure, 4.13, a distribution curve shows how the number of bitcoins given as rewards decreases over time. Given that Bitcoin is divisible by 8 decimal places, it is estimated that the last fraction of Bitcoin will be found around the year 2140.

Moore's law is based on the observation that computing power will double every two years. The Bitcoin distribution curve was planned to compensate for Moore's law.

To earn the mining reward, a miner must broadcast proof, called **proof of work**, that they have solved a difficult computing problem.

# Proof of work

Miners compete for the Bitcoin reward by submitting a "proof of work" to the network. Generating the proof of work involves the computation of a hash value on the block. The miner is looking for the smallest hash value possible.

The target value, called *difficulty*, is published by the network. If the hash value of the new block is less than the difficulty value published, then the miner has found a valid solution that is eligible as proof of work.

Blocks are accepted on the network as other miners confirm the proof of work.

# Confirmation

If another miner accepts the proof of work, the miner is awarded the new bitcoins and that block becomes the next block in the longest blockchain. All transactions grouped in the block are given a confirmation. All miners then start the process of mining on top of that chain.

As more blocks are added to the chain, the confirmation count for each transaction is increased. The more confirmations the transaction has, the more difficult it is to modify the chain of blocks.

 Although you can accept a payment with just one or two confirmations, it's highly recommended to have at least six confirmations to have mathematical trust that the transaction cannot be reversed.

However, if the transaction risk is very low, like paying for a cup of coffee, one can accept a payment with zero confirmations. There have been some efforts to build a statistical model to calculate the risk of accepting payments with less than six confirmations. From the model, the service provider can guarantee and insure the transaction.

# Difficulty level

As competition for the Bitcoin reward can vary, based on the number of miners on the network, the difficulty level can be adjusted to keep the reward rate at approximately once every 10 minutes.

The difficulty level is calculated from the rate at which the last blocks were accepted. If the rate of blocks found is less than 10 minutes, the difficulty will be increased; if it takes more than 10 minutes, it's decreased. The difficulty level is updated every 2,016 blocks.

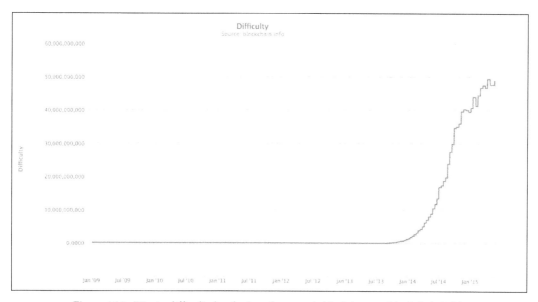

Figure 4.14 - Bitcoin difficulty levels since the genesis block (source: blockchain.info).

Shown in figure 4.14 is the network's calculated difficulty levels since the genesis block. Note how the difficulty level has dramatically increased in 2014 as the amount of competition has increased.

# Mining

When a node is actively searching for a hash value below the difficulty level, it is considered a miner. The actual process of mining includes listening for transactions to create the new block which is used to compute the hash value. Collectively, all the nodes on the network follow a basic workflow for mining:

- New transactions are broadcasted to the network. The nodes relay new transactions to the other nodes. New transactions are initially marked as *unconfirmed*.

- Each node collects and validates the transactions into a new block. The nodes continuously listen for new transactions and update the block as needed.

- Each node looks for the solution to a difficult problem that involves computing a hash of the block. The solution to the problem includes finding a hash value that's less than the published target.

- If a solution is found, it's broadcasted to the network. The solution consists of the block of transactions and the hash value. The proof is easily verified by the other nodes on the network.

- If all the transactions in the block and its hash value are valid, the block becomes the longest chain. All miners begin mining on top of that chain and the process is repeated.

# Solving a difficult problem

The goal of every miner is to produce a block of transactions with a hash value that's lower than the difficulty level published by the network. It would be extremely unlikely that computing the very first hash of a block of transaction will produce this hash value.

To allow another try, the Bitcoin protocol allows the miners to add a *nonce* to the end of the transaction, which is ignored by the network.

The nonce is a simple number that is incremented for each try. Each increment of the nonce results in another unique hash value. Since the hash values can be radically different from just a single character change, a large range of values is generated.

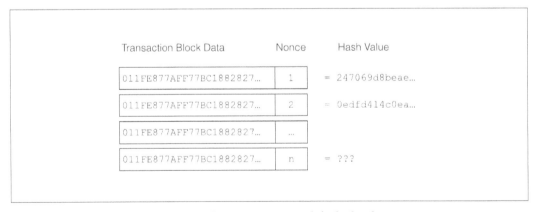

Figure 4.15 - Using a nonce to search for hash values

As shown in figure 4.15, the same transaction block data is used multiple times with an incremental nonce value. Each iteration of the nonce produces a unique and random hash value. The miners simply compute a hash for each sequential nonce until a hash is found which is less than the difficulty level.

Mining is highly competitive. In the beginning, it was common for a laptop computer to solve the puzzle. Today, however, it requires special hardware that can perform billions or even trillions of hashes per second.

Included in the new block is a Bitcoin address created by the miner. Once a valid hash value is found, the block is broadcasted to the network. If accepted, the new block becomes part of the chain and the new bitcoin reward is officially minted. Coins are generally accepted, after 100 blocks, as money that is available to spend.

As mining is highly competitive, large groups of mining pools exist. A mining pool consists of hundreds or even thousands of nodes that join together to earn a mining reward. If any node in the pool wins a reward, it is split up to the whole pool divided by the amount of computing power each node provided.

# Transaction fees

Transaction fees are small amounts paid to the miner for confirming your transaction. In some cases a fee is not required, but by paying a fee you are contributing to the incentive to mine.

The fee requirements are based on a ruleset accepted by the network. One rule is used to prevent payments intended to spam the network. If your transaction is less than 0.01BTC then a transaction fee of 0.0001BTC is required.

A transaction fee can be required, based on the miner, if the transaction size exceeds 10,000 bytes. As illustrated earlier in the chapter, a transaction can include many inputs and outputs which are simply stored as bytes in a record. The total number of bytes is the total transaction size. A simple way to estimate the size of a transaction is by using the following formula:

*size_in_bytes = 148 \* number_of_inputs + 34 \* number_of_outputs + 10*

Lastly, transaction fees are used to prioritize old and high-value coins. Based on the inputs listed in your transaction, a function is used to calculate the average age by the size of the transaction. If it is below a specific threshold, then a fee will be required. To simplify the priority calculations, one can assume that a single bitcoin can be spent one day after receiving it without paying a fee.

To prioritize old and high-value coins, the wallet software calculates the value of all the inputs in bitcoin multiplied by its age. The sum of all the inputs is then divided by the total size of the transaction in bytes. If the result is less than 0.576, then a fee will be required.

Fees are deducted directly from the transaction, reducing the output total by the amount of the fee. There is no output allocated specifically for the transaction fee.

Rules for requiring a transaction fee are shared similarly between the miners. However, each miner has the option of choosing which rules to implement. It is possible for a miner to accept any valid transaction without a fee. However, the majority that require a fee can delay or ignore transactions that bypass the fee structure. Therefore, to improve the chance of having your transaction confirmed as quickly as possible, it's best to follow the documented transaction fee structure.

# Network attacks

The Bitcoin network is protected by the consensus of the network. Valid transactions and changes to the software must be accepted by the majority of the miners on the network. Let's discuss the attacks that could occur:

# 51 percent attacks

It is theoretically possible for a large amount of computing power to overtake the network and accept double spending or prevent confirmations. This is called the 51 percent attack.

Although theoretically possible, the opposing argument to the attack notes the amount of computing power needed to perform the attack. Some argue that it is not financially feasible to execute the attack as the network could quickly reject the malicious blocks. It would be difficult for a large pool of nodes to produce a segment of the blockchain of more than six blocks in a row with a corrupt transaction.

# Race attacks

A malicious spender could try to double spend by broadcasting two transactions to the network at the same time. Given that the merchant would accept a transaction without any confirmation, it's possible to double spend in this way.

The quick antidote to this attack is to simply wait for confirmation of both the transactions.

# Finney attacks

The Finney attack is named after the Bitcoin developer Hal Finney. In this attack, a miner must pre-mine one transaction into a new block and spend the coins before releasing the block. If the payment is still unconfirmed, the new block will include a double spending transaction. The solution is to wait for at least six confirmations.

 Hal Finney is also known as the first person to have received a Bitcoin payment. He is credited with creating the first *Proof of Work* system. He worked through an illness that left him paralyzed until his death in August of 2014. `http://en.wikipedia.org/wiki/Proof-of-work_system`.

# Alternative coins

The Bitcoin software is open source and available to the public. From the public repository, many "alternative coins" have been created by copying the source code and re-configuring specific parameters. Each *alt-coin* can implement a different ruleset independent of any other *alt-coin*.

Generally, alt-coins implement different quantities for the total money supply or different block rates. For example, **Litecoin** has a total supply of 84 million coins and a mining rate of approximately two minutes.

Other alt-coins may implement a built-in inflation. For example, **Friecoin** has a built-in demurrage that's 5 percent per year. Basically, if you hold 1 Friecoin, it will be worth 5 percent less if you spend it one year later. This was used as an incentive to promote spending.

As another interesting coin, **Namecoin** uses its blockchain to record information about the ownership of names. The most popular use for this mechanism is to record the ownership of domain names. Using the Namecoin blockchain, one can earn Namecoins by mining and using the coins to purchase one's own `.bit` domain name.

The world of alt-coins is changing rapidly, with many new ideas being tested. Yet, it is not uncommon to see the rise and fall of new alt-coins. One should investigate the size and history of any alt-coin before investing.

We will explore alt-coins in detail later in the book.

# Summary

The blockchain is quickly proving to be a very impressive technology for recording the transfer of money. Due to its decentralized design, it is extremely resilient and completely transparent. It will continue to be a powerful force in the financial world as it develops over time.

In the next chapter, we'll set up and install our own Bitcoin node.

# Installing a Bitcoin Node

5

*"Right now Bitcoin feels like the Internet before the browser."*

*– Wences Casares, founder and CEO of Xapo*

Bitcoin was officially launched to the public with the release of its first client, Bitcoin-QT. The software is a fully functional Bitcoin node and implements the necessary functionality to bootstrap the Bitcoin network.

 Since version 0.9.0, it has been renamed Bitcoin Core.

In this chapter, we will set up and install our own copy of Bitcoin Core, the official client. Several other fully functional clients exist, but we'll use the official client in this chapter. Through the process we will cover the following areas:

- Understanding a Bitcoin node
- Installing Bitcoin Core
- Using Bitcoin Core
- Executing Bitcoin operations

## Understanding a Bitcoin node

Satoshi Nakamoto first released the Bitcoin whitepaper in October of 2008. Shortly after that, he released the first software implementation of a Bitcoin node. The software functions as an independent node that connects other nodes. On account of how it connects to the network, we will often refer to the software as the **client**. With a centralized network design, we often hear the terms *client* and *server*. Clients make a connection with a server to submit requests and to post data. As a classic example, an internet browser functions as a client that connects to a server to retrieve a webpage.

Bitcoin uses a decentralized network design. There is no central server to connect to, rather, clients connect directly to other clients. Nodes then broadcast or relay messages between themselves.

The client was open sourced to the world in 2009, allowing developers to independently improve the source code. Through online discussions, developers are able to coordinate bug fixes and improvements to the software. Revisions are tested and validated, and, if accepted, they are released to the official repository.

Initially, Satoshi Nakamoto contributed to the discussions but later disappeared. His early involvement with the development was crucial for the core team to understand the technology.

# Bitcoin Core

Originally called **Bitcoin-QT**, the official Bitcoin client is named **Bitcoin Core**. When installed, a service is started called **bitcoind**. Bitciond implements the protocols needed to connect to the Bitcoin network. Once connected to the client's user interface, Bitcoin Core can respond to the user input and perform actions such as broadcasting the transactions.

Bitcoin Core is publicly available on Github, a service that hosts public and private repositories of code. The Bitcoin Core source code is available at `http://github.com/bitcoin/bitcoin`.

Github is a source code repository service. The service implements a git server which manages and stores the source code and tracks the developers' contributions.

Developers run a client to push/pull their changes. *Branching* allows a developer to make changes to a parallel version of the source code. This allows them to experiment with various changes. The changes can then be merged back with the original branch.

Many developers have "forked" the source code to build their own versions of Bitcoin. The source code version control software, called **Git**, allows users to *fork* the source code. Forking the source code produces a new branch that separates its set of changes from the original branch. These changes can then be managed by a separate team of developers for their own use. Most of the new alternative coins were started as forks of Bitcoin.

Forking source code allows developers to merge commitments from various branches. Changes that are useful for other developers can be shared and merged between the branches. By selectively merging the commits, a software project can progress rapidly, as it can choose from a variety of submissions.

Today, the Bitcoin Core project has over 8,000 commits, selected from over 300 active developers.

# Internals of a node

Once connected to the Bitcoin network, independent nodes can participate in processing Bitcoin transactions. To function as a valid Bitcoin node, a client will often perform the following operations:

- Finding and connecting to other nodes
- Exchanging transactions with other nodes
- Exchanging blocks with other nodes
- Validating and exchanging transactions
- Maintaining its copy of the blockchain
- Managing private keys and a Bitcoin wallet (optional)
- Displaying a user interface (Bitcoin-QT/Core)

## Node discovery

To connect to a decentralized network, a node must first discover a list of the other active nodes. The primary piece of information necessary is the IP address or the domain name of the node. Usually, the client comes with a list of root nodes or *well known* nodes that can handle lots of connections. From there, various algorithms are used to find and share the list of active nodes on the network. The lists are actively maintained by the nodes and are freely shared.

A node is connected to the network as soon as a connection is open between it and another node. Connections to other nodes can be used to increase its bandwidth to the network. Typically, the client can open and maintain 6-10 connections.

Once connected, the node will be able to freely exchange messages with the Bitcoin network.

# Messaging

Once connected to the peer-to-peer network, nodes can send and receive transaction messages. This is the basic foundation from which all the Bitcoin operations are able to function.

New messages are broadcasted to each connecting node. If the node is able to respond, a message is sent back and processed by the client. Nodes can also relay messages to other nodes. For example, when a transaction is broadcasted to a node, it will validate and store the transaction. Then it will rebroadcast the transaction to all its connecting nodes. In effect, a transaction can be fully propagated through the network in only a few seconds.

Nodes also use messaging to exchange and relay validated blocks. Sharing blocks is how a node is able to construct a local version of the blockchain.

# Maintaining a Blockchain

By design, each node must validate and maintain its own version of the blockchain. Through this process, nodes are able to form a consensus about which version of the blockchain is the most valid. This is indicated by the length of the chain.

When a new client is initially installed, it has to reconstruct and validate the longest chain before it can validate new transactions. To catch up to the longest chain, the client requests each block, one by one, with the nodes it's connected to. Connected nodes with a current blockchain are then able to share their blocks with the client.

The client always performs a validation on the block and its transactions before accepting the chain.

# Transaction relaying

New transactions are programmatically sent to a node. The node validates the transaction against its local blockchain, checking for signatures and bitcoin balances. When accepted, the client adds the transaction to its list and then broadcasts it to all the connecting nodes.

Connecting nodes then validate the transaction against their blockchain. If valid, the node then broadcasts the transaction to all its neighbor nodes. The exponential effects result in the quick propagation of the transaction throughout the network.

# Bitcoin wallets

On top of the basic network operations, the client also maintains a Bitcoin wallet for the user. The wallet is able to generate unlimited addresses to send and receive the Bitcoin transactions. The private keys for each address are stored and encrypted by password.

When sending a payment, the client is able to combine multiple addresses as inputs to fulfill a payment amount. The client also generates an additional address for the change amount. Before sending the transaction, the client will prompt for the user's password and sign the transaction with the private keys.

We will demonstrate this process both with the graphical user interface and by hand using the command line interface.

# Installing the client

Bitcoin Core is publicly available for free from the official Bitcoin site (`www.bitcoin.org`). Installations are available for Windows, Mac, and Linux.

Figure 5.1 - Downloading the client

You can download the client from `https://bitcoin.org/en/download`. The site gives detailed instructions on how to install the client on each operating system (Windows, OS/X, and Linux).With the client installed, you'll be able to execute commands on the network using command-line scripts or with other development tools.

# Requirements

Due to the heavy use of processing and storage, several requirements must be met for proper performance:

- **At least 100GB of storage is recommended**: The client will need to download the entire blockchain and validate it locally on disk. Today, the blockchain size is about 50GB. This will grow at a linear and predictable rate.

- **Adequate bandwidth is necessary for performance and accessibility**: Some administrators may block ports on the network. Without access to the other nodes, the client will not be able to function properly, or at all. Make sure port `8333` is open.

- **Network speed should be sufficient and stable for proper performance**: Most home networks have high download speeds with slower upload speeds. The client will best serve the network if it has higher upload speeds.

- **It is desirable to have the node operating continuously for the best performance**: The node can only operate efficiently if it is in sync with the longest blockchain. Downtime of the node delays in blockchain synchronization leading to delayed operations.

- **The client may cause antivirus software to block access**: Make sure that you configure your antivirus software to allow access to port `8333`. Be aware that your node may become an attack target simply by being part of the network. One type of attack may deny service to your node for a period of time.

- **Finally, check the legal aspects of your jurisdiction**: Some users may be forbidden from using alternative forms of currency. Operating a public Bitcoin node could lead to legal notice or confiscation of equipment.

 Wikipedia has more information on Bitcoin legality by country, at `http://en.wikipedia.org/wiki/Legality_of_bitcoin_by_country`.

# Starting the client

When opened the first time, the client will ask you to confirm a location for your data. The client will use that location to store the blockchain and your wallet.

It is not required that you back up the full blockchain. Only your wallet file should be encrypted and backed up. Later, we will explore how to properly back up your wallet specifically without the blockchain data.

Figure 5.2 - Select a storage location with at least 50GB of available space

After the setup, the client will start running. Its first task is to search for other nodes on the Bitcoin network.

# Connecting to the network

Once started, the client will begin searching for nodes to connect to. If you meet the network requirements, this should be a quick task for the client.

Figure 5.3 - Bitcoin client status bar showing connection status and synchronization progress.

As shown in figure 5.3, the client has a status bar showing connection status as a set of bars. The colors red, yellow, and green are used to indicate the connection quality. Quality is measured by the number of connected nodes, and the bandwidth rates.

If your client can't connect, make sure that you check your antivirus software, firewall, and network conditions. Check with the administrator that you have the required network access.

# Downloading the blockchain

After its first installation, Bitcoin Core could take several days to download the full blockchain. It is best to keep the computer running continuously in a cool environment.

 The client will use lots of processing power to validate the blocks, which will often generate lots of heat. Without sufficient ventilation, the computer can quickly overheat, leading to a shutdown or physical damage of the equipment.

Some operations will not be available until the full blockchain has been synchronized. For example, current balances cannot be verified without a full blockchain. Therefore, the client will not be able to process any new transactions.

# Using the client

Once started, you'll be prompted with the **Overview** screen. As shown next in figure 5.4, the **Overview** shows your current balances, the amounts pending, and any recent transactions.

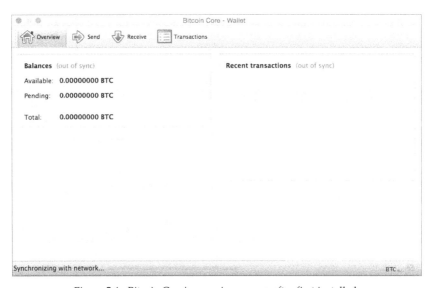

Figure 5.4 - Bitcoin Core's overview screen after first installed.

Before receiving any Bitcoin, you should be familiar with some basic preliminaries to help protect your Bitcoin wallet.

# Encrypting your wallet

When first installed, your wallet will be stored unencrypted on the disk. Malicious software can access your wallet and steal the private keys. To protect your wallet, you'll need to encrypt it with a passphrase, or a long password.

By selecting **Encrypt Wallet** from the **File** menu, you will be prompted to enter a new password. After you set it, you can change it by selecting **Change Password** under the same menu.

> Be sure to protect your password. There is no recovery mechanism. Losing your password will result in the loss of your bitcoin.
>
> As a tip, you could back up your wallet before encrypting it. Make sure that you protect it in a secure location. With an unencrypted copy, you can recover your wallet in case you lose your password.

# Backing up your wallet

Bitcoin Core automatically creates a pool of 100 new addresses which are used to receive bitcoin. When sending bitcoin, the client may also use an address for the change address of a transaction. You should regularly backup your wallet, especially if you've used the 100 addresses from the initial pool.

If you are using automated backup software, you can include just the `wallet.dat` under the location provided during the installation. It is not necessary to backup the blockchain data as it can be downloaded again.

> Before accepting any bitcoin in your wallet, make sure that you have a backup saved in a location not on your computer. If your `wallet.dat` file becomes lost or corrupt, you will not have access to your private keys.

To restore your wallet, simply copy the backup file to the location used to store your Bitcoin data. During the initial setup, the system prompts you to confirm the location. By default the locations are:

- **OS/X**: `~/Library/Application Support/Bitcoin/wallet.dat`
- **Windows XP**: `C:\Documents and Settings\username\Application data\Bitcoin\wallet.dat`

- **Windows Vista and 7**: `C:\Users\username\Appdata\Roaming\Bitcoin\wallet.dat`
- **Linux**: `~/ .bitcoin/`

# Balance and history

Referring back to figure 5.4, we can find our balances and transaction history. The **Available** balance includes all the confirmed transactions. Any unconfirmed transactions are listed under **Pending**.

 Note that, in the client, the bitcoin amounts are shown in BTC by default. You can change the unit by opening **Preferences...** under **OS/X**, or **Settings | Options** on Windows. In the **Options** dialog, you have a choice between BTC, mBTC, or µBTC.

# Receiving transactions

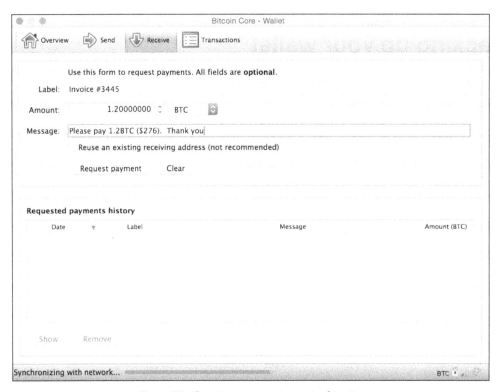

Figure 5.5 - Creating a request to receive bitcoin.

Shown in figure 5.5 is the request screen. Requests to receive bitcoin can be initiated here and later sent as an e-mail or posted on a website.

Starting at the top, the **Label** field is used to set an **Account**, which can contain multiple Bitcoin addresses. Accounts are useful for grouping multiple addresses together. Balances are maintained separately by the account. Later in the chapter, we'll discuss how to list accounts along with their addresses and balances. Labels will appear in the receiver Bitcoin client when prompted to pay.

The **Amount(BTC)** field is the number of bitcoin to received, optionally in units of BTC, mBTC, or μBTC.

The **Message** field is sent along with the request, and will also appear in the receiver's Bitcoin client.

You can optionally choose to reuse an existing Bitcoin address. This is not recommended for most requests. To keep your bitcoin as anonymous as possible, it's recommended that you use a new address for each payment. If selected, you'll be prompted to choose an address from your wallet.

When submitted, your request will appear in a window, as shown in figure 5.6:

Figure 5.6 - The bitcoin request form

The payment request window automatically displays a QR code, which can be scanned by a mobile Bitcoin wallet.

The URL can be copied and pasted, and sent via an email to your recipient. When clicked, their default Bitcoin wallet software will open, repopulated with the amount and the message.

The URL can also be embedded on a webpage as a hyperlink. Simply copy and paste the URL into an anchor link:

```
<a href="bitcoin:16ZZypJ7MZQqqwZAC5uaN7Ng6bRWzDcjJZ?amount=2.3">
```

The history of your requests is displayed below the entry form. The history gives you access to the previous requests. Removing a request from the list does not remove the Bitcoin address from your wallet.

# Sending transactions

Figure 5.7 shows the send payment screen. Note how we can specify multiple recipients based on Bitcoin addresses. Each address can be assigned a specific label and amount.

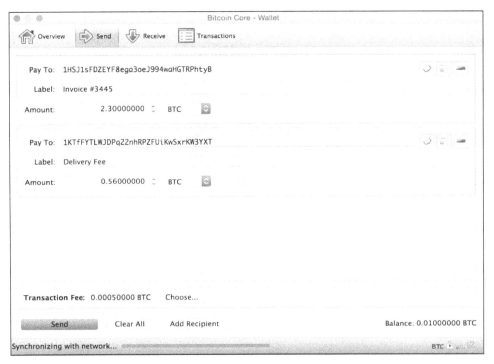

Figure 5.7 - Send Bitcoin payment screen.

If the Bitcoin address you enter already exists in your wallet, the label will be repopulated with the address's account.

You can change the parameters for the transaction fee by clicking on the **Choose...** button next to the transaction fee amount.

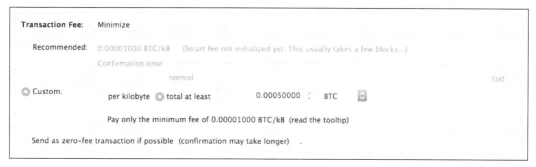

Figure 5.8 - Transaction fee parameters

The default option is set to **Custom**, which specifies a fee based on a fixed amount or the size of your transaction. This can be useful if you have a large or complex transaction.

The recommended method for calculating a fee analyzes the most recent transactions. Using statistics based on the fees paid and the time needed to confirm, an algorithm is able to suggest an amount.

# Executing Bitcoin operations

Bitcoin Core has a **Console** which allows you to execute commands directly. The backend engine, called **bitcoind**, will execute the command and interact with the wallet, the blockchain, or the network, as requested. The results are returned as standard JSON text.

JSON stands for **Javascript Object Notation**. Developers can use the JSON format as a way of encoding data that's easily read by both humans and computers. Following is an example of using JSON to describe a company and address:

```
{
    "title" : "ACME Manufacturing",
    "address" : "1234 Main Street, Anywhere, CA"
}
```

Curly braces, { }, are used to group key/value pairs. Keys are used to reference a piece of data. Each pair is separated by a colon, ":". JSON uses quotes, "", to define strings of characters.

Bitcoin Core accepts and responds with JSON.

# Opening the console

To open the window, select **Debug window** under the **Help** menu, and then select the **Console** tab. You will be prompted with a window similar to the example shown next in figure 5.5.

The console accepts the commands from the input box on the bottom. Results are displayed above. Pressing the up or down arrow will scroll through the history of the commands entered.

Clicking on the minus button will clear the history. It is useful to do this after executing sensitive commands involving private keys.

At any time, you can type the following command:

```
> help
```

A list of commands, as shown in figure 5.5, will be displayed. Each command will have listed its accepted parameters.

We will explore the console with some basic commands to manage our wallet.

Figure 5.5 - Bitcoin Core's Debug window accepts commands

# Working with an encrypted wallet

If your wallet has been encrypted with a password, you'll have to provide the console with the password in order to execute the commands against your wallet:

```
> walletpassphrase "your-password" 600
```

The command `walletpassphrase` will validate your password and use it for the number of seconds specified, 10 minutes in the preceding example. The console will prompt you for the password after the time specified has passed.

If you would like to encrypt a new wallet, simply execute the following command:

```
> encryptwallet "your-password"
```

To lock your wallet again, you can execute the following command:

```
> walletlock
```

Update your password by executing the `walletpassphrasechange` command:

```
> walletpassphrasechange "oldpassphrase" "newpassphrase"
```

Once opened, you can access your wallet's info:

```
> getwalletinfo
```

The command will return several metrics on your wallet, including its available balance:

```
{
  "walletversion" : 60000,
  "balance" : 0.00000000,
  "txcount" : 0,
  "keypoololdest" : 1433284498,
  "keypoolsize" : 101,
  "unlocked_until" : 0
}
```

To access just your balance, use the following command:

```
> getbalance
0.00000000
```

# Working with Bitcoin addresses

Once you have access to your wallet, you can manage the Bitcoin addresses and their private keys within your wallet. Bitcoin Core maintains a pool of addresses used to send and receive bitcoin. To generate a new address, simply run the following:

```
> getnewaddress
1Mc1ws7Jq9giGdNNtbA2asFjAj4dxnsvqz
```

To view the private key of the address, execute the `dumpprivkey` command:

```
> dumpprivkey 1Mc1ws7Jq9giGdNNtbA2asFjAj4dxnsvqz
KzwfuMZw6fq9uZLrDeVSECfcaEYeGQSXc4JpCmoQ2G4eYMHVJ8Ht
```

 When a password is set on the wallet, the private keys are always encrypted. To access the keys, you will always be required to provide a password. However, inspection of some of Bitcoin Core's data files will show your public addresses listed in plain text.

Bitcoin addresses are grouped into **Accounts**. The default account is just an empty string, noted as " ". Some commands require an account to be specified. In our examples, we'll use the default account, " ".

**Accounts** are used to group your Bitcoin addresses. By grouping the addresses, you can send money from a specific set of addresses.

By default, all the addresses are created under an account with the empty title, " ". To assign your address to a specific account, use `setaccount`:

```
> setaccount ''1MHT4tit3Nas3RnejfgmZWZBTY23k4CEwp'',
  ''account-name''
```

To display a list of all the accounts and their balances, execute the `listaccounts` command:

```
>listaccounts
{
  "" : 1.30000000,
  "Personal" : 2.34000000,
  "Savings" : 120.3345770000
}
```

You can list all the addresses using the `getaddressesbyaccount` command. We'll list the addresses in the default account as follows, " ".

```
> getaddressesbyaccount ""
[
"1CbcUGpQ4cx6DrnuJ1Jx8UyD8g6EPCcs4",
"1Mc1ws7Jq9giGdNNtbA2asFjAj4dxnsvqz",
"1MHT4tit3Nas3RnejfgmZWZBTY23k4CEwp"
]
```

To retrieve the balance of a Bitcoin address, we can use the `getreceivedbyaddress` command. The command accepts an address and an optional confirmation count. Transaction confirmations have a variable interval, with the average being around 10 minutes.

Bitcoin Core will only include a transaction in the balance if a sufficient number of confirmations have been made.

To check the balance immediately after a transaction was sent and prior to any confirmations, we can execute the following:

```
> getreceivedbyaddress 1BQGrTbpp7RnPrSVMXbQ1j9kCf71DZBtfC 0
0.01000000
```

Retrieving Transactions

To view a list of transactions from all the addresses, simply execute the following:

```
> listtransactions
[
  {
    "account" : "",
    "address" : "1BQGrTbpp7RnPrSVMXbQ1j9kCf71DZBtfC",
    "amount" : 0.01000000,
    "vout" : 0,
    "confirmations" : 554,
    "blockhash" : "0000000000000000003079ed4b12dd0…",
    "txid" : "ca6383333a3640e7c6564d6702a3cd5bbef2e…",
    "time" : 1433891570,
    ...
  }
]
```

Note that in the result, a transaction ID is provided by `txid`. This is a hash of the actual transaction. It uniquely identifies the transaction and can be used to retrieve the transaction at a later time.

To retrieve a single transaction, use the `gettransaction` command:

```
> gettransaction ca6383333a3640e7c6564d6702a3cd5bbef2e…
```

# Creating and sending a transaction

To send bitcoin from the console, we'll need to gather some information about the outputs we'll be using to fund the transaction.

To fund our new transaction, we'll start by listing all the Bitcoin addresses that have an unspent balance from a previous transaction. From our list we can choose which address, or addresses, to use as the input.

# Generating a destination address

To start, let's create a new Bitcoin address that we can use to send a small amount of money back to ourselves. Normally, this will be your recipient's address.

```
> getnewaddress
1MWJRUPkfaXpAPLSn7pZfVxdSNXZfmN9Uo
```

You can list a number of destination addresses. To keep this example simple, we'll limit ourselves to just one.

# Selecting a funding source

To fund the transaction, we'll need to select the outputs from one or more transactions that contain an unspent balance. As described in *Chapter 4, Understanding the Blockchain*, the inputs to a new transaction always reference a previously confirmed transaction.

Using the `listunspent` command, we can view the possible funding sources for our new transaction:

```
> listunspent
[
  {
    "txid" : "ca6383333a3640e7c6564d6702a3cd5bbef2ea5e38…",
    "vout" : 0,
    "address" : "1BQGrTbpp7RnPrSVMXbQ1j9kCf71DZBtfC",
    "account" : "",
    "scriptPubKey" : "76a91472180ee34a0b1a7661eb0d176cb0ccc63a…",
    "amount" : 0.01000000,
    "confirmations" : 554,
    "spendable" : true
  }
]
```

From the results we can see that we have a Bitcoin address with a balance of 10mBTC (0.01BTC). We will use the `txid` to select this transaction as a funding source to our new transaction.

# Specifying a change address

The full balance of the address we're referencing has to be spent. Therefore, we will have to create a change address in our wallet to hold the unspent balance. In our example, we'll send only 2mBTC to our new address. We will send the remaining amount to the new change address:

```
> getnewaddress
14egKB8ybvRupSAgsA17Z5Gr17yadaHuKA
```

# Including a transaction fee

The last aspect of our transaction is the small miner's fee. We'll send a small fee to the miner. The amount of the transaction fee will be 0.5mBTC. We'll use the following table to illustrate the anatomy of the transaction:

| Inputs | | | Outputs | |
|---|---|---|---|---|
| 1hvzSo… | 0.01BTC | | 1MWJRU… | 0.0020BTC |
| | | | 1MJZH5E… | 0.0075BTC |
| Totals | 0.01BTC | | | 0.0095BTC |
| | | | | |

Note the small difference in the amounts between the inputs and the outputs. The unaccounted amount of 0.5mBTC will be paid to the miner whose confirmed block is accepted by the network.

# Defining the transaction in JSON

Next, we'll have to create a small snippet of JSON to define our transaction for the console. Starting with the input, we'll reference the txid from our unspent transaction:

```
[
  {
    "txid" : "ca6383333a3640e7c6564d6702a3cd5bbef2e…" ,
    "vout" : 0
  }
]
```

The value vout refers to a sequential index, starting with 0, and is unique for each input. Thus, if there was a second input defined, the vout value would be 1.

Next, we'll list the address that will receive our bitcoin:

```
{
    "1MWJRUPkfaXpAPLSn7pZfVxdSNXZfmN9Uo": 0.002,
    "14egKB8ybvRupSAgsA17Z5Gr17yadaHuKA": 0.0075
}
```

For clarity of illustration, we've expanded the JSON by brackets and tabs. However, we'll need to collapse it down into one line without the tabs and the breaks.

# Encoding and signing the transaction

The next step will involve creating an encoded version of the transaction. With an encoded version of the transaction, we can apply a digital signature.

Using the command `createrawtransction`, we'll encode the transaction so that the network can interpret it. The command accepts two JSON parameters, the input and the output we previously defined. We'll have to wrap them in `'''` and specify it on one line:

```
> createrawtransaction '''[{"txid" :"ca6383333a3640e7
c6564d6702a3cd5bbef2ea5e380670bd2e5fc2bce1ee6ac3","vo
ut" : 0}]''' '''{"1MWJRUPkfaXpAPLSn7pZfVxdSNXZfmN9Uo":
0.002,"14egKB8ybvRupSAgsA17Z5Gr17yadaHuKA": 0.0075}'''
0100000001c36aeee1bcc25f2ebd7006385eeaf2be5bcda302674d56c6e740363a33
8363ca0000000000ffffffff02400d0300000000001976a914e0ed1f2593a7314e4d0
0fe6b8eea8e2617c70af488acb0710b00000000001976a914280895c791b2e923f070
e05199ed4f7b16416f4988ac00000000
```

The transaction is compiled into a hex format that can be easily shared with the Bitcoin network. However, this transaction is unsigned and will be rejected by the nodes.

To sign the encoded transactions, we'll first have to make sure that we have access to the private keys by providing the console with our encrypted wallet's password. If your wallet is unencrypted, you can skip this step.

```
> walletpassphrase 'your-password', 6000
```

Now, we can sign the encoded transaction with the `signtransaction` command (note that the text has been abbreviated):

```
> signrawtransaction 0100000001c36aeee1bcc25f2ebd7006385ee…
{
"hex" : "0100000001c36aeee1bcc25f2ebd7006385eeaf2be5bcda302674d56c6e74
0363a338363ca000000006b483045022100c09b5f830aacaeba474c5d5c018a20204
a05afb78fd2759ba5db1f7476e6fc8302202332922f9effcb972023da8ed4facdae24
d341e9901f48e637edf93e8a358bfe0121026f3ac6ee47afb4f52ef6ccfcd43b4b9caf
```

```
3d4fd97a9fb22970f532c608e9f825afffffffff02400d0300000000001976a914e0ed1
f2593a7314e4d00fe6b8eea8e2617c70af488acb0710b00000000001976a914280895c
791b2e923f070e05199ed4f7b16416f4988ac00000000",

"complete" : true
}
```

Note the **complete** key. In our example, it's set to `true`, meaning that we've successfully signed the encoded transaction. If your result is `false`, check to make sure that you have the necessary private keys in your wallet and that your passphrase has been set.

## Reviewing the transaction

Now that the transaction has been signed, it's ready to be broadcasted to the network.

Before sending the encoded and signed transaction, we can run a simple command to verify the details.

Using the `decodetransaction` command, we can see how our transaction is configured. We will execute the command with the hex codes from the `signrawtransaction` results:

```
> decoderawtransaction
0100000001c36aeee1bcc25f2ebd7006385eeaf2be5bcda302674d56c6e740363a338
363ca000000006b483045022100c09b5f830aacaeba474c5d5c018a20204a05afb78fd
2759ba5db1f7476e6fc8302202332922f9effcb972023da8ed4facdae24d341e9901f4
8e637edf93e8a358bfe0121026f3ac6ee47afb4f52ef6ccfcd43b4b9caf3d4fd97a9fa
a970f532c608e9f825afffffffff02400d0300000000001976a914e0ed1f2593a7314e4
d00fe6b8eea8e2617c70af488acb0710b00000000001976a914280895c791b2e923f07
0e05199ed4f7b16416f4988ac00000000
{
  "txid" : "e953e6b6c69f158d2710d1b3436257a1bd2a063...",
  "version" : 1,
  "locktime" : 0,
  "vin" : [{
    "txid" : "ca6383333a3640e7c6564d6702a3cd5bbef2e...",
    "vout" : 0,
    "scriptSig" : {
    "asm" : "3045022100c09b5f830aacaeba474c5d5c018aafb78...",
    "hex" : "483045022100c09b5f830aacaeba474c5d5c018a202...",},
    "sequence" : 4294967295}],
  "vout" : [{
    "value" : 0.00200000,
```

```
      "n" : 0,
      "scriptPubKey" : {
        "asm" : "OP_DUP OP_HASH160
e0ed1f2593a7314e4d00fe6b8eea8e2617c70af4 OP_EQUALVERIFY
OP_CHECKSIG",
        "hex" : "76a914e0ed1f2593a7314e4d00fe6b8eea8e2617c70af488ac",
        "reqSigs" : 1,
        "type" : "pubkeyhash",
        "addresses" : ["1MWJRUPkfaXpAPLSn7pZfVxdSNXZfmN9Uo"]}}, {
      "value" : 0.00750000,
      "n" : 1,
      "scriptPubKey" : {
        "asm" : "OP_DUP OP_HASH160
280895c791b2e923f070e05199ed4f7b16416f49 OP_EQUALVERIFY
OP_CHECKSIG",
        "hex" :
"76a914280895c791b2e923f070e05199ed4f7b16416f4988ac",
        "reqSigs" : 1,
        "type" : "pubkeyhash",
        "addresses" : ["14egKB8ybvRupSAgsA17Z5Gr17yadaHuKA"]}}]}
```

Note the `scriptPubKey` key. That's the digital signature of the transaction. Using this signature, the nodes can verify that this transaction was signed with the original key(s) of the listed inputs.

# Broadcasting the transaction

We are now ready to broadcast the transaction to the network. We can simply use the `sendrawtransaction` command (note that the encoded transaction has been shortened for readability):

```
> sendrawtransaction "0100000001c36aeee1bcc25f2ebd7006385e..."
e953e6b6c69f158d2710d1b3436257a1bd2a063e7cb3db4580cab69d23bd0397
```

The command will return the `txid` of our newly submitted transaction. At any time, we can use that value to reference our transaction:

```
> gettransaction ae74538baa914f3799081ba78429d5d84f36...
```

Figure 5.11 - Our newly broadcasted and unconfirmed transaction.

Bravo! Our newly created transaction has been broadcasted to the network and will be confirmed shortly.

> Other services are available to help decode and push transactions to the network. For example, `blockchain.info` provides these features.
>
> To decode a raw transaction, simply open `https://blockchain.info/decode-tx`.
>
> To broadcast a transaction, open `https://blockchain.info/pushtx`.

# Summary

In this chapter, we explored how a Bitcoin node operates on the network. We installed Bitcoin Core, the official client, and used it to send and receive money. Lastly, we learned about some basic operations and how to execute them programmatically by hand.

In the next chapter, we'll explore the Bitcoin mining process.

# 6
# Understanding the Mining Process

*"We have elected to put our money and faith in a mathematical framework that is free of politics and human error."*

*– Tyler Winklevoss, Entrepreneur*

The Bitcoin network distributes newly-minted bitcoin through a novel approach called **Mining**. By voluntarily supplying raw computing power, miners serve the network by validating and confirming Bitcoin transactions. In return, the miners are awarded bitcoins from a limited supply. Along with each award, they collect fees included with the transactions they choose to validate.

Bitcoin mining, an important aspect of the network, is highly competitive and involves many technical factors. In this chapter, we will explore the mining process in more detail. With this base understanding of the process, we will be able to understand the feasibility of mining.

In this chapter, we will discuss the following topics:

- Explanation of the mining ecosystem, mining pools, and available hardware
- Setting up a mining client
- Connecting to a mining pool
- Introduction to tools to help calculate the feasibility of mining

# Digital gold

The first humans certainly had an advantage with regards to finding precious materials such as gold and silver. It's easy to imagine flakes or small nuggets of gold naturally exposed by streams and lakes. Human beings walking around the area could easily collect them for trade or utility.

As time went on, more and more of the easily available precious metals and gems were picked. Miners continued their search deeper and deeper into the earth, risking their lives and wealth in search for these valuable materials.

With the expansion of human civilization to new lands and continents, new sources were found. In 1849, gold was found in a stream near Coloma, California. After the news broke, hundreds of thousands of miners, called the *49ers*, rushed out to California in search of the gold.

Within a few years, most of the easily found gold was picked, driving the miners to use more advanced techniques. By the mid 1850s, the miners had adopted hydraulic mining equipment and other mechanical means to extract the gold. It was a difficult process and successful mining required skill and luck.

# Bitcoin mining

The 1849 California Gold Rush is analogous to the beginning of Bitcoin's mining story. They both share similar characteristics.

First, both gold and bitcoin have a limited supply. The amount of gold on the planet is fixed and cannot increase. Similarly, Bitcoin's algorithm is designed to ensure that only a fixed amount of bitcoin will be found.

In both cases, the early miners had better results mining in the beginning. In the case of the 49ers, within the first 2 years much of the gold found was easily picked from streams and rivers. With Bitcoin mining, the number of bitcoins awarded to the miners decreases over time. The new reward block halves every 4 years and the mining difficulty increases, as it's adjusted every two weeks based on the competition to mine. Thus, many early adopters were able to easily mine more than 50 bitcoins a day using a standard computer with a fast computer or a graphics processor.

Today, mining for gold is an expensive operation and is generally left to large mining companies funded by large investments of capital. The same holds true for Bitcoin. Large mining companies and pools exist, driving the competition to find bitcoin way up.

The golden years of Bitcoin mining may be behind us, but the process of mining still plays an important role in the Bitcoin ecosystem. In addition to earning newly minted bitcoins, the miners also earn transaction fees. These fees are paid by the sender of a bitcoin transaction and create an incentive for the miners to quickly confirm their transaction.

Having a large base of miners is important to Bitcoin as it builds trust in the network. The larger the base of miners, the more difficult it is to overtake the network. As we've seen with many of the alt-coins that have been released, without any significant base of miners, there's very little trust in the currency. Ultimately, it yields a low exchange rate with little demand for the currency.

Let's begin by exploring the various aspects involved with mining a bitcoin.

# Exploring the mining ecosystem

Bitcoin mining provides the network with two very important processes: the creation of new bitcoin and the confirmation of transactions.

As discussed in *Chapter 4*, *Understanding the Blockchain*, the miners listen for new and valid transactions to combine them into a new block. The block represents a scope around a group of transactions that can be easily validated against the previous blocks. Structuring the ledger this way makes the processing of transactions easy to distribute.

From the perspective of the miner, a new block is potentially valuable. The bytes from the block are used as the base for computing an answer to a difficult computing problem. The miners make many millions of attempts at solving the difficult computing problem in hope of finding the solution before any other miner.

If found, the miner quickly broadcasts the solution to the network to make the claim. If it is confirmed by the network, the miner receives the new bitcoin, as well as all the fees included with each transaction in the block. The new block then serves as the latest block in the blockchain. The miners then start the race again by listening for new transactions and repeating the process. The following Figure 6.1 summarizes the process:

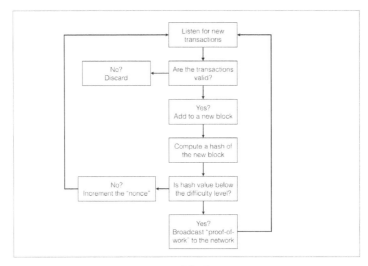

Figure 6.1 - A summary of the Bitcoin mining process

# Validating transactions

Each transaction broadcasted to the network must be checked for double spending, that is, sending more bitcoin than what's available, and for a valid digital signature. To confirm the available balance, the miner must have a validated copy of the entire blockchain.

As described in *Chapter 5, Installing a Bitcoin Node*, after installation, a client will connect to the network and begin requesting each block sequentially from the other nodes on the network. After checking each block against the previous blocks, one by one, the blockchain is replicated and stored locally.

The local copy of the blockchain contains every transaction from the beginning of time. This ledger is maintained and used to validate the spending balance of each new transaction. If a transaction is found to be invalid, it is simply ignored and discarded.

The second check requires validation of the digital signature. Using cryptographic algorithms, the miner is able to check the signature attached to the transaction to validate the integrity of the transaction. Any modification to the transaction will result in an invalid signature, and thus the miner is able to confirm that the transaction to be processed was the original version sent from the holder of the private key.

With a list of valid transactions, the miner assembles a new block and uses it as the base for solving a difficult computing problem.

# Proof-of-Work

In *Chapter 4, Understanding the Blockchain* we described a **hash** as the result of a mathematical function applied to a set of data. In our case, the data is the new block of valid transactions. When a hashing function is applied to the data, a numerical value is returned. If we change any byte of the data and recompute the hash, we'll get a completely new hash value that's radically different to the original.

Mining involves using the hash function to generate a hash result. If the hash result matches the target, it's considered the solution. If the result is invalid, a throwaway number called a **nonce** is added to the data. The data set is then hashed again, giving the miner another try. This process is repeated until a solution is found.

When a solution is found, it's broadcast to the network as a new block, which also contains the difficulty target and the winning nonce. This is called **proof-of-work**. The other nodes on the network can recompute the hash on the block and the nonce to verify the proof-of-work.

If accepted, the new block becomes part of the blockchain. The nodes that agree on the solution then share the new block with the other nodes on the network. The end result is that the new bitcoins and the transaction fees collected are awarded to the winning miner.

# SHA-256

Computing a hash value is computationally expensive. To produce the proof-of-work, the hashing function is executed many times until a valid hash is found. Thus, the work is described as "solving a difficult computing problem".

Bitcoin uses a hash function called *SHA-256*. It's a secure cryptographic hash function that can computed by software or more efficiently by hardware.

Specifically, the miners are looking for a hash value that's less than the target value. They will perform many millions of hashes per second looking for the winning hash result. Since any small change to the data set produces a different hash value, a nonce is added to the set. Each retry of the hash includes an increment to the nonce. When incremented, the resulting hash is completely different to the previous hash. This gives the miner another chance at finding a hash value that's lower than the published difficulty level.

Illustrated next in figure 6.2, the block data, consisting of valid transactions and a nonce, is hashed many times until a hash value is found that is less than the difficulty level:

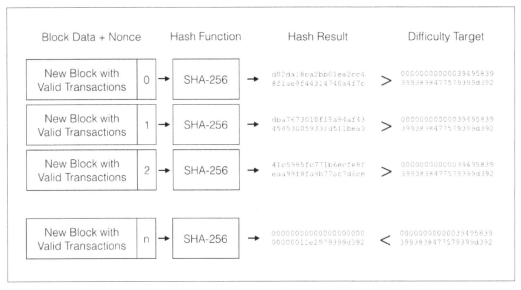

Figure 6.2 - Mining involves incrementing a nonce to generate a hash until a solution is found.

In figure 6.2, we can see that the same data from the block is used with an incremented hash to compute the hash values. Using a **brute force** approach, the miner makes many millions of attempts to find **n**, the nonce that produces the winning hash result.

# Scrypt

Litecoin, as well as many other alt-coins, uses a different configuration for the hashing algorithm. Scrypt also uses SHA-256 for hashing, but with an additional algorithm called Salsa20, which requires a large amount of memory, or RAM, to compute. Thus, the scrypt algorithm is not only computationally expensive; it's memory intensive as well.

The rationale behind using an additional component, in this case, a large amount of RAM, is to make it harder to scale the mining process using computer processors alone. This gives those with access to individual computers an advantage over the mining operations that scale with processors.

# Mining rewards

Newly minted bitcoins are awarded for proof-of-work confirmed by the network. The number of bitcoins awarded is set on a curve, which halves every 210,000 blocks.

The first rewards were set at 50 bitcoins. After approximately four years, the first 210,000 blocks were mined and the reward was reduced by half to 25. The rate will continue halving, to 12.5, 6.25, and so on, until the last fraction of a bitcoin is found. The total number of bitcoins is fixed at 21,000,000 and the smallest fraction is 0.00000001.

[  The smallest unit of Bitcoin is called a **Satoshi**, named after its developer. ]

The curve, which declines in half over time, is intended to offset the anticipated increase in available computing power. In other words, as the cost of computing power decreases, the difficulty of earning the reward increases to balance the equation.

# Difficulty metrics

As competition for the rewards increases, the rate of solutions found to the difficult computing problem will increase. With more miners searching for the solution, the average rate could become less than the intended rate of one new block every 10 minutes.

To offset this, a *difficulty level* is calculated and adjusted every 2016 blocks. The calculation considers the last two weeks of transactions to produce a target difficulty. If the average is below the 10 minute average, the difficulty is increased, and if it is above, the difficulty is decreased (source: `https://en.wikipedia.org/wiki/File:Difficulty.svg`).

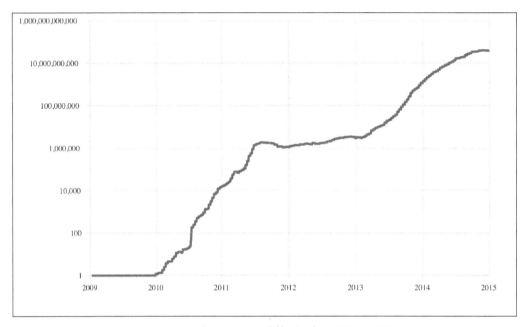

Figure 6.3 - Relative mining difficulty from 2009 to 2015

Using the difficulty metrics, a miner can make some basic predictions about how much computing power will be required to mine a single bitcoin.

These are some quick facts to remember about the Bitcoin mining process:

- Approximately every 10 minutes, a block reward is found
- Every two weeks, the difficulty level is adjusted
- Every four years, the block reward is halved
- Only 21 million bitcoins will be found

Circa 2015, over 60% of all bitcoins have been mined, with the current block reward set at 25.

# Mining hardware

In Bitcoin's early days, standard CPUs were used to compute the hashes. Included in the original Bitcoin client was a feature that allowed you to use the CPU to mine. In the early days of Bitcoin, it was easy for a single CPU to earn a full award of bitcoin. However, as the number of miners increased, CPUs quickly became obsolete for mining.

As mining competition increased, software was adapted to utilize graphic processing units (GPUs). GPUs are optimized to perform mathematical operations many times faster than CPUs. They are used to accelerate the computation of complex graphics applications such as gaming and rendering. Because of their optimizations, they are well suited to performing the mathematical operations needed to quickly compute a hash.

The mining operators often maintained racks of GPUs. Several graphics cards could be connected to one computer. This resulted in the generation of large amounts of heat. To maintain peak performance of the equipment, air conditioning units were required to keep it cool.

Soon after the GPUs were adopted as the standard for mining, computer chip manufactures began developing microchips that performed the hashing computations directly. This resulted in a large increase in the number of hash performed per second, with a fraction of the electricity needed.

Initially, **Field-Programmable Gate Arrays**, (**FPGAs**) were configured and used for building the mining rigs. These are special integrated chips that allow a programmer to encode the hardware level instruction to be executed directly on the chip. They provided the miners with fast hashing speeds and used much less electricity.

**Application Specific Integrated Chips** (**ASICs**), quickly became the hot item for mining. These chips could perform billions of hashes per second while using far less power.

In the beginning, the technology was brand new and in high demand. ASIC vendors often accepted large amounts of pre-orders while anticipating a successful delivery.

While some vendors were able to deliver on their promises, others were unable to, resulting in major losses for some customers.

Buyers should be careful with placing pre-orders. Always research new vendors and their claims.

In the following table 6.1, the various types of mining hardware are listed with their performance statistics:

| Hardware | Performance (hps = hashes/sec) | Power (Watts) |
|---|---|---|
| CPU | 1–50 million hps | 150–300 watts |
| GPU | 100–800 million hps | 500–1000 watts |
| FPGA | 100–800 million hps | 5–40 watts |
| ASIC | 10,000–1,000,000 million hps | 200–600 watts |

Table 6.1 - Performance by available Bitcoin mining hardware

Referring to the table 6.1, one can see how the performance per watt has dramatically decreased with the introduction of the ASIC mining equipment. ASICs can have a wide variance in both performance and power consumption, so upfront costs and hashes per watt are important to consider.

In Bitcoin mining, all the CPU and GPU, and most FPGA, processors have been replaced by the ASIC mining hardware. Due to the competition and the costs involved, mining with anything other than an ASIC is not viable.

# Mining conditions

Due to the demands placed on the equipment, it's crucial that it be kept and maintained in a proper environment to sustain conditions for peak performance.

Most notable are the cooling requirements. Air conditioning may be required to maintain a constant temperature for the equipment to operate. Make sure that you factor a cooling system into your budget and design.

Electricity usage from both the equipment and the cooling must be assessed and arranged. Clean and stable electricity is important so as to not damage the equipment. Electrical spikes and high loads can cause interruptions to your mining operation.

Constant monitoring of the equipment is important. Downtime could result in a much lower return on investment than anticipated. Thus, it is common for serious mining operations to have a full time staff to monitor the conditions and maintain the equipment.

# Mining pools

It can be quite difficult for a single ASIC miner to find the necessary proof-of-work to earn the rewards from a new block. This is especially true if every miner on the network is working individually as well. Thus, the chances of earning the bitcoin are either all or nothing with regards to a single block reward. To improve the chances of earning the bitcoin, a strategy for mining called **pooling** exists.

The mining operators are able to join together their collective power to form mining pools. As a group, their chances of finding the difficult to generate proof-of-work become much better. Upon winning the reward, the pool agrees to share the profits based on the work contributed by the individual miners.

Mining pools give lower powered miners an advantage because it can be very difficult for them to earn a full block alone. When operating as part of a collective, their computing power is awarded based on the amount of computing power provided.

## Mining shares

In a pool, the work is measured in **shares**. One share is issued for each proof-of-work submitted. However, in the case of a mining pool, the proof-of-work is accepted based on the easiest difficulty level.

At the easiest difficulty level, a much larger range of nonces are eligible as the solution to the computing problem. Proof-of-work generated against an easy difficulty level is how the individual miners are able to prove to the pool that they have been working.

Eventually, when a share meets the network's difficulty level, the whole pool earns the reward, as it is divided and distributed to the individual miners based on the shares submitted.

## Fees and Payout

The mining pools charge fees, typically ranging from 0.5 percent to 3.0 percent, depending on the payout method. Based on the payout methods, the mining pool operator may be at risk from a miner who cheats about the share reported. Generally, the more risk the mining operates assumes, the higher the fees.

A **round** is usually used in the calculation, and represents the current block being mined. After a new block has been found, the round is closed and another is started.

Payout from the mining operator is based on various methods. Some methods are optimized for quicker payouts, while others give incentives for new shares. The various methods are designed to reduce or prevent cheating. The mining pools use different methods, along with completive fees, to encourage miners to join their pool.

Some common payout methods are listed in the following table 6.2:

| Payout | Description |
|---|---|
| Proportional | The block reward is paid to all the miners in proportion to the number of shares found. |
| Pay per share | The miners are paid for each share submitted. The amount paid depends on the current difficulty. The pool operator assumes the risk. Therefore, the fees paid to the pool tend to be the highest. |
| Score | A proportional reward weighted by the time submitted. Later shares are worth much more than earlier shares, based on a weighted score by time. |

Table 6.2 - Common mining pool payout schemes

# Cloud mining

Mining contracts are available for those who wish to outsource the mining process to another company. Companies offering **Cloud Mining** services allow one to purchase a contract for a specific amount of time and hash rate. The service operates similarly to the mining pool process.

The advantages of cloud mining are obvious, as the buyer doesn't have to own the equipment, maintain it, and mange its uptime. All the equipment is based in a remote data center and is maintained by the cloud mining company.

However, the buyer must beware. The returns on profit can be much lower than a normal investment. Furthermore, there have been scams reported and losses from malicious companies. Make sure that you do your research on a service before paying for any services or contracts.

# Estimating profitability

There are many factors involved in estimating mining profitability. The significant variables are hardware costs, electricity, and mining difficulty.

# Hardware efficiency

Starting with the hardware, one must consider the hashing speed of the equipment against the power used. A simple formula for evaluating the mining efficiency would consider these two variables:

*Hashes per second / power consumption = efficiency*

Hardware efficiency calculations are useful for evaluating the hardware. Be aware that the hash rates published by the vendors could vary from the actual rates. Additionally, it may take some time for the equipment to arrive. Make sure that you do some research on the forums to see what hash rates the other customers are getting.

# Factoring in the difficulty level

One must compare the difficulty rate against the available hardware to project an estimate of the possible returns. Using some simple math, the rewards from mining at a specified hash rate can be estimated.

We start with the hash rate:

*hashes = number of hashes per second*

Given that there are 86,400 seconds in a day, we can calculate the number of hashes per day:

*hashes * 86400 = hashes per day*

The chance of a hash being a valid share is approximately one in 2^32:

*(hashes * 86400) / 2^32 = shares per day*

Factoring in the difficulty level, we can estimate that the shares' chances of being the solution to a new block is as follows:

*(hashes * 86400) / (2^32 difficulty) = blocks per day*

Finally, we apply the block reward:

*(hashes * 86400 * reward) / (2^32 * difficulty) = average bitcoins per day*

Using the formula, we can make a quick estimate of the average number of bitcoins we can earn per day, based on some published hardware statistics.

For example, given today's difficulty level, 49,692,386,355, and a block reward of 25BTC, we can estimate the return of a high performance ASIC miner.

Using the Spondoolies SP35 Yukon for our example, its listed performance is 5.5 tera-hashes. Thus, the average daily return would be as follows:

*(5500000000000 \* 86400 \* 25) / (2^32 \* 49692386355) = 0.05566301499 BTC*

This is only an estimated bitcoin return, based on the difficulty and the hashing rate. For a more elaborate estimate of mining profitability, one would also include the hardware costs, the electricity rates, and the maintenance costs.

## Selecting a currency

When looking to estimate profitability, it's important to consider the crypto-currency with the best chances of making a profit. Difficulty level and exchange rate are the two important variables involved.

With over 500 alt-coins in existence, a miner has a large set of options to choose from. To help with analyzing the data, one can rely on some tools to help with the calculations.

Coinwarz (`www.coinwarz.com`) is a useful site for evaluating profitability across the various crypto-coins. As shown in the following figure 6.5, one can easily select and compare the statistics across the various currencies and provide sort parameters based on different exchange rates:

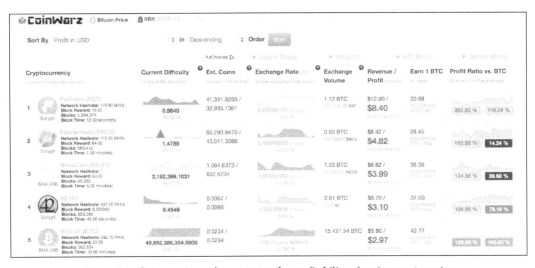

Figure 6.4 - Coinwarz is used to compare the profitability of various crytpocoins

Coinwarz maintains difficulty statistics, exchange rates, and volumes, and uses them to give a historical view of profit rations. Using this information, one can make an educated guess about the various trends happening between crypto currencies and optimize their chances for an investment in mining.

# Exchange rates

The current exchange rate for the currency you are mining is an unpredictable factor in calculating mining profitability. Many miners have an optimistic view of Bitcoin for the long term, yet in the short term the volatility leads to uncertainty with mining investments.

Given the risks, we can still make some broad assumptions and use calculators to give us a range of returns.

The Coinwarz website offers some useful tools for calculating future earnings based on hash rates, difficulty, electricity costs, and block rewards. Referring to our previous example with the SP35 Yukon, we can project an estimated annual return, as illustrated in the following figure (`http://www.coinwarz.com/calculators/bitcoin-mining-calculator`):

## Estimated Expected Bitcoin Earnings

The estimated expected Bitcoin earnings are based on a statistical calculation using the values entered and do not account for difficulty and exchange rate fluctuations, stale/reject/orphan rates, and a pool's efficiency. If you are mining using a pool, the estimated expected Bitcoin earnings can vary greatly depending on the pool's efficiency, stale/reject/orphan rate, and fees. If you are mining solo, the estimated expected Bitcoin earnings can vary greatly depending on your luck and stale/reject/orphan rate.

AdChoices ▷      ► Calculator      ► PayPal Bitcoin      ► Bitcoin Mining      ► Bitcoin Miner

| Time Frame | BTC Coins | USD | Power Cost (in USD) | Pool Fees (in USD) | Profit (in USD) |
|---|---|---|---|---|---|
| Hourly | 0.00231929 | $0.56 | $0.30 | $0.00 | $0.26 |
| Daily | 0.05566301 | $13.47 | $7.20 | $0.01 | $6.26 |
| Weekly | 0.38964110 | $94.29 | $50.40 | $0.05 | $43.84 |
| Monthly | 1.66989045 | $404.10 | $216.00 | $0.20 | $187.89 |
| Annually | 20.31700047 | $4,916.51 | $2,628.00 | $2.46 | $2,286.05 |

Figure 6.5 - Coinwarz's Mining Calculator

# Setting up a mining client

After doing the proper analysis of costs and return on investment, one may decide if it's the right time to proceed with setting up a mining operation.

## Requirements

In general, you'll need to have the proper conditions to set up a basic mining operation. To start with, we'll briefly cover the essentials: capital, hardware, facilities, and availability.

## Capital

Most return on investment calculations for Bitcoin mining show profitability over a period of time, exceeding one year. The assumption made for the projection includes a stable exchange rate and difficulty level. However, these two factors often vary, which can seriously affect the actual profits.

Essential to starting a mining operation is sufficient capital to carry the operation forward. Before starting the venture, make sure you have enough capital to cover the costs for at least 1 to 2 years, based on the various projected conditions.

## Hardware

The purchase of hardware is one of the more volatile aspects of mining. Hardware vendors are constantly designing and improving their equipment. Often, new equipment is pre-sold with several months of backorder time.

Without high-performance hardware, one cannot begin mining. Thus, be sure you have access to a decent set of equipment before securing the rest of your mining operation.

Another aspect to consider when purchasing equipment is the future value of the equipment based on its performance and operational life. Bitcoin mining equipment is changing rapidly and can be outdated within a year. After its useful life is finished, you may have to resell the equipment or recycle it in order to upgrade to new and more powerful equipment.

This was the unfortunate result of a large surge in miners buying the GPU cards. Large orders of GPUs were purchased and used to mine, but when the ASIC chips arrived, the GPUs were quickly replaced. Many miners ended up with large quantities of hardware unusable for mining Bitcoin. Much of the equipment was used for mining other alt-coins or sold.

Remember, an important aspect of one's mining operation is being constantly up to date with the latest vendors and releases.

## Facilities

Early mining enthusiasts started their mining operations from their homes, often in spare bedrooms, garages, or basements. These operations quickly grew into racks and racks of equipment, with fans constantly running as make-shift cooling systems.

The sustainability of these operations running from a personal residence or a family dwelling quickly diminishes. Therefore, it's important to secure a permanent place to set up your mining racks with proper ventilation and cooling.

Easy access to the hardware is important. The ability to diagnose and replace the equipment helps to ensure maximum uptime of your mining operation. Also, one should consider the future expansion of their mining operation. Be sure to plan ahead with space if you plan to grow your operation.

Your mining facilities should include a stable and clean power supply. The mining equipment will pull a constant wattage. Thus, it's important to ensure proper power lines, connections, and outlets to provide adequate wattage.

With all the equipment running at full speed, the sound volume and vibrations can be an issue. Make sure to consider planning for sound proofing the facility if excessive noise is an issue for the neighbors.

Finally, make sure that your facilities are properly protected from theft and other environmental factors, such as flooding and/or earthquakes. It may be possible to have the facilities and its equipment insured. Be sure to check with your agent.

While mining hardware can operate continuously without interruption, a quick response from its operators is important to manage uptime. Hardware and software failures can happen at any time. Without a quick response, the downtime can seriously affect the profitability.

Therefore, it's important to be able to monitor your operations with a quick response time. It is advisable to have a partner or a small team on staff to provide backup or to cover shifts.

In October 2014, an online publication called Motherboard gained access to a large Bitcoin mining operation based in China. The short documentary uncovers many aspects involved with the mining operation and can give some insight to mining on a massive scale. The video is available online at `http://motherboard.vice.com/read/chinas-biggest-secret-bitcoin-mine`.

# Choosing the equipment

Procuring high-performance equipment is crucial to the success of your mining operation. As an important aspect of your business, you should research the latest vendors and their equipment.

ASIC miners start in price at around $2,000 and can easily pass $8,000. In addition to the cost of the hardware, you should factor in the equipment's mining efficiency. As mentioned earlier in the chapter, divide the hash rate by the wattage to estimate the equipment's efficiency.

Personal USB ASIC miners are available within the price range of $40 - $100. They are capable of mining a few Satoshis in a reasonable amount of time, but are considered non-competitive in the market. They can make an interesting project for experimentation and learning.

Another metric often used in evaluating equipment's efficiency is *Mhash/J* or millions of hashes per joule. One joule of energy is equal to one watt of power used for one second. Hashes per joule can be used to evaluate the efficiency over time.

Online reviews of vendors and equipment are available. The Bitcoin wiki has some general information that one can use to begin. Refer to `https://en.bitcoin.it/wiki/Mining_hardware_comparison`.

Make sure to factor in the crypto-currencies you're most interested in mining. Many alt-coins use Scrypt and cannot be mined by most ASIC hardware. You'll have to do some research depending on the currency, its difficulty level, and the hardware available to mine it.

# Choosing the software

Once you have your hardware purchased and setup with a computer, you'll need to setup the mining software.

The mining software will manage connecting to a mining pool and interacting with the hardware. Part of the process is assigning work from the mining pool to your mining equipment and reporting the shares back to the pool. The two most popular packages are `cgminer` and `BFGMiner`.

Cgminer supports ASIC and FPGA Bitcoin mining, and is available for Windows, OS/X, and Linux. It supports connecting with multiple mining pools. You can download the source code from GitHub (`https://github.com/ckolivas/cgminer`). Provided with the source code are instructions on how to setup and install the software. Also provided are examples of how to connect to the hardware and the mining pools.

BFGMiner also supports ASIC and FPGA Bitcoin mining and is available for Windows and Linux. It can be downloaded from its website at `http://bfgminer.org`.

With your hardware and software set and ready to work, the next step would be to connect to a mining pool.

# Connecting to a mining pool

There are many options available for joining a mining pool, depending on your preferences. You should make an educated decision on which mining pool to use, based on the payout method, the fees charged, and how often a block reward is found. Other features that are nice to have include statistics, easy withdrawal of funds, and various types of merged mining.

# The payout method

The payout method can vary between the mining pools. Check the method and the fees included to make sure they match your risk and ability to wait for payouts. Depending on your mining operation's availability, the type of payout may affect your rewards. For example, the miners who do not run stable mining operation will be **punished** using a **score** based payout. This means that if your miner gets disconnected for some time, your score may drop to zero.

Also, consider the terms for the payout. Some mining pools release earnings automatically, while others may impose a threshold.

# The pool fees

Some pools may charge a fee. The amount usually depends on their assessment of risk and the features they offer. Generally, paying no fees is best, but in some cases paying a fee could mean better chances of earning a block reward. For example, Deepbit charges 3 percent fees but pays for every solved block, even it becomes invalid.

# The pool speed

The number of rewards earned by a pool is directly related to the overall pool speed. The faster the hash rate for the pool, the more blocks found. In the long term, the rate of rewards found will average out, but with smaller pools you could wait days or weeks to receive a payout.

# Additional features

After identifying the payout method, the fees, and the speed that best suits your needs, you can evaluate the pool's additional feature set. Some pools offer nice graphs and statistics, or e-mail notifications and alerts.

Listed next in table 6.3 are the top Bitcoin mining pools. Also listed are the payout methods used:

| Pool Name | URL | Payout Method | Speed (Ph/s) |
| --- | --- | --- | --- |
| Antpool | `antpool.com` | Pay per last N shares, 0% fee<br>Pay per share, 2.5% fee<br>Solo, 1.0% fee | 74.72 |
| Eligius | `eligius.st` | Capped pay per share, 0% fee | 11.96 |
| BitcoinCZ | `mining.bitcoin.cz` | Score-based payouts, 2% fee | 10.62 |
| GHash.io | `ghash.io` | Pay per last N shares, 0% fee | 9.3 |
| BitMinter | `bitminter.com` | Pay per last N shifts, 1% fee | 3.03 |

Table 6.3 - Popular Bitcoin mining pools (speed is measured in peta hashes / sec)

# Avoiding large pools

The larger the pool size, the more concern there is for it to approach the theoretical 51% attack size. Although there is some debate about how effective the attack would be, the large pools can quickly raise concern in the community.

Generally, miners have more incentive to not join a large pool as it diminishes the overall value of the network. Since the miners are working to earn bitcoin, they have an interest in keeping the network functioning properly.

There was a case, early in 2014, in which the mining pool GHash.io reached 42% of the network. As the pool size was approaching 51 percent, many miners began voicing the issue and the need to reduce the pool size. Within 24 hours, many miners had left the pool, bringing the size back down to 38 percent.

# Running the client

Once your account is setup with the mining pool of choice, you can quickly configure your mining software to connect to the pool and start the mining process.

Assuming you've installed `cgminer`, simply execute:

```
cgminer -o http://pool:port -u username -p password
```

The software will start by connecting to the pool. If everything checks out, the mining software will begin issuing work to your mining equipment, as shown in figure 6.6 (source: `http://hashfast.com/cgminerscreenshots/`):

```
cgminer version 3.1.0 - Started: [2013-06-04 01:09:38]
-----------------------------------------------------------------------
(5s):1.933M (avg):1.908Mh/s | A:105400  R:1472  HW:0  U:6.6/m  WU:1748.2/m
ST: 2  SS: 121  NB: 6623  LW: 102837  GF: 11  RF: 0
Connected to us.wemineltc.com diff 198 with stratum as user bmoconno.bamt
Block: 1d5fe800f56d3d7b...  Diff:46.7M  Started: [01:25:25]  Best share: 45.8M
-----------------------------------------------------------------------
[P]ool management [G]PU management [S]ettings [D]isplay options [Q]uit
GPU 0:  79.0C 3589RPM | 599.6K/601.4Kh/s | A:33184 R:356 HW:0 U:2.09/m I:19
GPU 1:  72.0C 3178RPM | 639.2K/637.7Kh/s | A:35289 R:543 HW:0 U:2.23/m I:20
GPU 2:  73.0C 1682RPM | 670.0K/669.6Kh/s | A:36927 R:573 HW:0 U:2.33/m I:20
-----------------------------------------------------------------------

[2013-06-15 01:26:19] Accepted 899958eb Diff 2.78K/198 GPU 0 pool 1
[2013-06-15 01:26:21] Accepted 3edb5326 Diff 229/198 GPU 0 pool 1
[2013-06-15 01:26:21] Accepted 04a7075c Diff 3.12K/198 GPU 0 pool 1
[2013-06-15 01:26:28] Accepted 00a993bd Diff 352/198 GPU 1 pool 1
[2013-06-15 01:26:37] Accepted 389a60c2 Diff 583/198 GPU 1 pool 1
[2013-06-15 01:26:50] Accepted 5b3087fd Diff 338/198 GPU 1 pool 1
[2013-06-15 01:27:14] Accepted a52674b2 Diff 462/198 GPU 2 pool 1
[2013-06-15 01:27:21] Accepted acb9d49f Diff 226/198 GPU 0 pool 1
[2013-06-15 01:27:23] Accepted 0abb2fa6 Diff 689/198 GPU 1 pool 1
[2013-06-15 01:27:24] Accepted 42644b8b Diff 349/198 GPU 1 pool 1
```

Figure 6.6 - cgminer running, showing statistics and block updates

# Summary

Mining Bitcoin can be a complicated yet rewarding venture. In this chapter, we covered many aspects of planning and setting up a mining operation. Yet, it's important to remember that conditions for profitability are constantly subject to change as this new field of technology develops and matures.

In the next chapter, we're going to look at how to program Bitcoin and explore some interesting areas with digital contracts.

# 7
# Programming Bitcoin

*"I am very intrigued by Bitcoin. It has all the signs. Paradigm shift, hackers love it, yet it's derided as a toy. Just like microcomputers."*

*– Paul Graham, Creator of Yahoo Store*

Bitcoin, as a currency, exists and functions according to its underlying technology, the Blockchain. The Blockchain is built from a global network of computers. Each miner acts as an autonomous unit with an economic incentive to confirm transactions. The Blockchain's basic unit, the transaction, is an extensible unit upon which we can develop new types of applications.

In fact, each transaction is simply a small script which transfers control of some fraction of a Bitcoin from one address to another. With each transaction, a small amount of data can be stored. When the scripting language is combined with **transaction metadata**, other types of more complex operations can be written, executed, and stored.

Furthermore, an entire platform can be built on top of the Blockchain. Programmers can define new scripts and operations that run on top of the existing Blockchain operations. These operations are executed and confirmed in the same way as ordinary Bitcoin transfers. The end result is a platform that is completely decentralized, transparent, and resilient.

In this chapter, we will write a set of scripts to illustrate how we can *program Bitcoin*. We will cover the following topics:

- Installing BitcoinJS
- Programming common Bitcoin operations
- Sending and receiving transactions

- Creating multi-signature addresses
- Scripting a decentralized escrow contract

The projects listed in this chapter involve computer programming. Although a basic understanding of programming is assumed for working with the projects, curious readers are welcome to browse through the examples shown to develop awareness of what Bitcoin and the Blockchain can deliver, and to get a glimpse of the new types of applications that are now possible.

# Programmable money

In our modern day society, many aspects in our life are managed or controlled by computer software. From the alarms on our cell phones that wake us up, to the lights that direct the traffic on the way to work, to all the ways we stay connected to each other—software drives it all. The ability to program daily life has transformed our culture and society at a phenomenal rate.

Before software, information was static and often recorded on paper. For example, at a typical financial company, the information had to be counted, sorted, and hand-compiled to extract meaningful knowledge from it.

Today, computers quickly compile these reports, giving the analysts an inside perspective into the business in real time. Software allows the programmers to script operations that can be repeated, often millions of times a second. We can't imagine running a business today without the support of software.

Furthermore, entire industries are created by financial software systems. Financial analysts rely on more and more advanced and complex software to find an edge in a highly competitive marketplace.

In today's world, we still rely on banking, financial services, and government agencies to protect and regulate our financial industry and markets. Yet, even with the best intentions, there is still corruption, manipulation, and fraud. The costs of these inefficiencies are ultimately passed down to the customer or the merchant.

With Bitcoin, and the invention of the Blockchain, we can imagine the next big step in finance: programmable money. We are now finding ourselves at an interesting point in time. Through the intersection of technology, economics, and cryptography, we now have the ability to maintain a completely decentralized system, secure and resilient, yet publicly accessible, from which we can build new types of applications.

Complex financial operations can be scripted, executed, and protected by the Blockchain with minimal costs and without any third-party to trust.

# Decentralized applications

As powerful our modern day software systems are, they are still centralized and closed between entities. For example, the accounts listed in one company's system are rarely accessible by another company. Thus, intermediary services are required to maintain trust and accountability between the companies.

This barrier results in inefficiencies that can eventually lead to a breakdown of trust. The financial crisis of 2008 was largely built on top of a complex construction of financial instruments that were repackaged and resold. It was very difficult to assess the true risk of a package due to this complex arrangement.

The benefit of having a decentralized application in the financial world is the ability to have a transparent system upon which we can operate business between multiple entities without a trusted third party. Full transparency, without having to disclose an identity, is very lucrative to a global market where assets can be traded at real-time speed.

With the invention of the Blockchain, we arrange escrow accounts, open market places, and sign digital contracts without the need for an intermediary entity. The participants interact with the system with the private keys helping to protect their identity. The participants can rely on the Blockchain to keep the exchange fully transparent and locked forever. As opposed to paying large fees to financial services, this powerful technology is available for just a few pennies per transaction.

# Blockchains

Some organizations in the financial industry have expressed interest in the Blockchain technology aside from Bitcoin. They seek to implement the technology without the currency to leverage the benefits of using a transparent ledger. The potential lies in the ability to share accounts or contracts without a trusted third party. While this is possible, it does change the dynamics a bit.

Bitcoin was launched as a small network of nodes mining and confirming transactions. For the first year, the price of a whole bitcoin was less than a cent. With a small mining base, it would have been easy to overtake the network, but because the currency wasn't worth much, there was little incentive to do so.

Over time, as Bitcoin attracted new interest, the network quickly developed. The computing power of the network eventually grew with the price of the Bitcoin. A higher Bitcoin price attracted more miners, which made the network harder to overtake. Thus, the two actions converged, creating a powerful and valuable network.

Bitcoin's value and the network's computational power are deeply interconnected. This interconnectedness is what allows the participants to interact without a trusted third party.

## Public Blockchains

With a public blockchain, the miners have the liberty to come and go. There is an economic incentive for them to protect the network and contribute to consensus rather than to cheat or overtake the system. The value of the public blockchain's unit of account, in our case Bitcoin, is the driver behind the economic incentive.

As it turns out, attracting a strong network of miners is really difficult, which proves its intrinsic value. With a strong economic incentive, such as Bitcoin, it would be challenging to attract a public network of nodes whose interest is to protect the network.

## Permissioned Blockchains

A blockchain without Bitcoin, or any other unit of account, is possible with a different set of terms. Unlike an open blockchain, a trusted group of miners would need to be selected. The participants of the system would have to agree to trust the miners and the software they use to confirm the transactions. Blockchains that are closed to a select group of nodes are called **Permissioned Blockchains**, as each node must be accepted by the user base.

There may be situations where a permissioned blockchain could be useful. For example, a private group of participants would like to maintain a private ledger between them. In that case, they could elect a balanced group of miners between themselves, and execute their operations privately on the network.

## Smart contracts

Imagine a group of participants who would like to conduct business together without revealing their identity and without involving a third-party of trust. They could agree on a particular contract that can include an objective set of data points, such as an expiration date or a strike price.

The terms can be programmed as a script running on top of the Blockchain. Provided all the parties agree on the sources of the inputs, the system can follow through with the implementation, execution, and confirmation of the contract. The digital contract would be protected by the network.

The participants claim their stake in the contract with a public address, and hold the corresponding private key that permits them to act. Without having to disclose private information, the parties can agree to come together and conduct a transaction with contractual transparency.

Another example can include the transfer of ownership of digital property or physical property that is controlled by a digital key. Since the transfer of ownership is publicly available, smart contracts have the potential to reshape the role of the government and title companies.

> Ethereum (`http://ethereum.org`) is a complete platform with advanced scripting abilities that's designed to run as an independent blockchain. While still in development at the time of this writing, its promise is to deliver a full platform for building distributed applications.

Let's start by taking a tour of how we can build some basic applications with Bitcoin and the Blockchain. Then, later in the chapter, we'll write some scripts to build a digital escrow contract.

# Installing BitcoinJS

To begin our adventures in programming with Bitcoin, we're going to install and work with a set of development tools:

- **NodeJS**: This is a platform built on the open sourced Javascript engine from Google. It will allow us to write and execute the scripts quickly and easily. These scripts can be written to run in a Web browser or on a server.

- **BitcoinJS**: This is a Javascript library for working with Bitcoin and its cryptographic functions. We'll use BitcoinJS to generate private keys and addresses.

- **Blockchain.info**: This is a public API that will allow us to query the blockchain for balances, and to broadcast the transactions to the network. While we can implement our own Bitcoin node, as described in *Chapter 5, Installing a Bitcoin Node*, using Blockchain.info as the alternative allows us to get up and running quickly and easily.

# Requirements

To install the packages listed in the preceding list, you'll need a computer running Windows, OS/X, or Linux with at least 1GB of free hard disk space and 4MB of RAM.

It's recommended that you have some experience with working in a command line environment. The examples shown will involve working with commands that could vary between your operating systems. As a fair warning, some debugging may be necessary.

# Beginning the installation

We'll begin by installing NodeJS. Installer packages are available at `https://nodejs.org/download/`. Simply download the installer and follow the instructions for your operating system. When finished, restart your computer.

To test the installation, we'll run the simplest one line program, `Hello World`. First, open your computer's terminal and then enter the following commands:

```
~ node
```

You should next see the NodeJS prompt. Simply type the following command and hit enter:

```
> console.log("Hello World")
Hello, world!
undefined
```

Our one-line script writes the greeting to the display and tells us that the function returned an **undefined** value. We can ignore that part, but given that we've gotten this far, we can confirm that NodeJS is successfully installed. When you're ready to exit the prompt, press *Ctrl* + *C* twice in a row.

On Windows, you can access the command prompt by clicking **Start | Run** and entering `cmd`.

On OS/X, you can access the command prompt by pressing command + Spacebar and entering `terminal`.

Additionally, you can download and install custom terminals for Windows and OS/X.

Next, we'll install BitcoinJS by using **NPM**, also known as **Node Package Manager**. NPM is used to install and manage the Javascript modules. The modules are used to group the computer code so that it can be shared with the other developers or projects.

For our example, we'll install `bitcoinjs-lib`, which is a Javascript library for working with Bitcoin. The documentation and source code for the module is available at `http://bitcoinjs.org`.

To install BitcoinJS, we simply run NPM's `install` command with the `-g` flag to make it globally accessible on our computer:

```
~ npm install bitcoinjs-lib -g
```

For OS/X and Linux users, you may have to run as an administrator:

```
~ sudo npm install bitcoinls-lib -g
```

To test our installation, we can run the `node` again and enter the following command:

```
~ node
> var bitcoin = require('bitcoinjs-lib')
undefined
```

We are using the `require` function to load the module `bitcoinjs-lib` and assign it to the variable `bitcoin`. If everything goes well, we should get the `undefined` result and we can check this off our list.

# Editing the source code

Now that we have our development environment ready, we'll need to choose a text editor to write and save our scripts.

There are many applications available for all platforms. By default, Windows comes with Notepad and OS/X comes with TextEdit. These are simple applications with the most basic feature set, but are fine for our examples.

If you would like to use a more advanced editor, some fine options are as follows:

- **Sublime Text**: `http://www.sublimetext.com`
- **Atom**: `https://atom.io`
- **Notepad++ (Windows Only)**: `https://notepad-plus-plus.org`
- **Textmate (OS/X Only)**: `https://macromates.com`

Once you have the editor of your choice set up and installed, we can proceed by setting up a workspace for the scripts. The workspace is simply a folder for holding our scripts.

Simply choose a path that's easy to access and/or meets your preference. For example, you can start by creating a folder on your desktop named `learning-bitcoin`. When creating and editing the scripts, make sure to save them to this folder.

When working from the command line, we'll have to change the working directory to the location of our workspace, so that we can run the scripts. We can select a folder on the desktop with the `cd` command:

```
~ cd ~/Desktop/learning-bitcoin
```

Or from Windows Vista and 7:

```
> cd c:\Users\[user name]\Desktop
```

> If you're new to working from the command line, it may be helpful to find some online tutorials to become more familiar with the environment and the basic command needed to navigate it from your operating system.

# Programming common Bitcoin operations

Let's start by introducing `bitcoinjs-lib` by working with private keys and public addresses. The module provides us with some useful components for working with elliptic curve keys.

To generate a new private key, we'll start `Node.js` from our command line and enter the following commands:

```
~ node
> var bitcoin = require('bitcoinjs-lib')
> var private_key = bitcoin.ECKey.makeRandom()
> console.log(private_key.toWIF())
KzgRK4nN6bcb5iQN8tLL85U5anc84uH7G9KtsZuqU23h5fN7Z6v4
```

From our example, you can see that we're importing the bitcoinjs library and calling `ECKey.makeRandom()`, which returns a random private key. We store an `object` that represents the key in a variable called `private_key`. On the third line, we print out the key in WIF format to the console. The result is a valid key from which we can compute a public address from:

```
> console.log(key.pub.getAddress().toString())
149TUxVkJzowbNDwExc34t4EfyNgAL1pco
```

 **WIF** stands for **Wallet Import Format** and is used to make copying ECDSA keys easy to work with. The format has a built in checksum that helps to prevent mistyped characters.

For a more useful example, let's write a script that generates 100 keys in a format that we can import into Excel. Using your text editor, write and save the script to your work folder as `make-keys.js`:

```javascript
// make-keys.js
// Creates a comma separated file (CSV) of private keys and address
// Formatted for importing into a spreadsheet application

var bitcoin = require('bitcoinjs-lib')
var fs = require('fs')

// the number of keys to generate
var num_of_keys = 10

// the name of the export file
var file_name = "my-keys.csv"

var stream = fs.createWriteStream(file_name)
stream.once('open', function(fd) {
  for (var x=0; x<num_of_keys; x++) {
    var key = bitcoin.ECKey.makeRandom()
    var line = [x, key.toWIF(), key.pub.getAddress().toString()]
    stream.write(line.join(", "))
    stream.write("\n")
  }
  stream.end()
})
```

Then, from your command line, run the following commands to create your file:

```
~ node make-keys.js
```

If all went well, you'll have a file in the same folder named `my-keys.csv`, from which you can import into Excel:

| | | |
|---|---|---|
| 0 | L5ZDzaxFp6QJtEHN1TLFjKKpnMrAH3jztTR6KbsEMbcuUW9VUVkp | 1Fonn1wdDs3QNDDid4TzAcBps1RuJkEY9J |
| 1 | L1vQopLkDFodNh991AP1PwYsZosvT9n4HB8xvj771Wja28jj4dGc | 16B7os4ikkeCHxN9K1qgDAVHpRNy3vUupr |
| 2 | KztNWrkNJfiHVMsGbgRduYeKkNBraMNSWcqfq4X4F9tnAm6CBbzB | 1LUMP9Jq5qiHnvDCg6sCQ8KWNQwPYTQZcv |
| 3 | L1CBv9EXQacM5fZjJt9XtD79Cn8hjEizRfkmmHWPjtYG9otTNz2B | 1He1Suox2LBKrXfqdYFy7vPXAEPYVmn3JV |
| 4 | Ky8fZtQbF3U4PaSK4E3ohnFeyLCNJo55sD8krdYy3X4ZLj5bNUDj | 14U734m1ahkJdgSueM2oXkF3CLyxbnSZBD |
| 5 | KzESgPcwr32WfjSro98pVTDBKLxRyK6pWoMYKUEsJf6XvPUhPAFc | 1Mjipf7XNL2NJXdSKChQA5ncEdi8PmM6hw |
| 6 | L2nzecMKM4yS2KNBCRsD4F6wpBDhdg1yQcJYx9S58ygWZKTUF2xy | 1CVyNBLhYndkA2hHbFh2Ltqi8oAQRsLMzQ |
| 7 | KwXPxQeSxaP9TFyfyFM2SUiuEJkGc1kq8GKxAzzFdCJuLGvGbwbg | 1Krt6qR8JBQE2HvCU6PALKEsRAUfP6mNk8 |
| 8 | L1UpT7kXwai3fdSqE3arefEahom98nwPRpaMJht4EdhFCiihbmCp | 1DsYC5rFQYBwojS8agiua9HVxdjjc7JWM6 |
| 9 | KzWtJNMCPXXC547RNw6vL3ceF1jGBebatfsThdqeauxW6LkYC6du | 1FHkdKkuCVqAZ2u2vmG52e6MxcXpnsJE8D |

Figure 7.1 - The private keys and addresses generated from our script

 If you intend to use this script to generate private keys to hold real bitcoin, make sure to protect your file from theft, spyware, or loss. Safeguard your keys before using any of the addresses.

# Checking your balance

To check the balance of a single Bitcoin address, we'll have to query the Blockchain. We'll use Blockchain.info's API to get real-time balances in our script. For a limited rate of queries, we can use their API for free, without the overhead of setting up our own Bitcoin node, and have our scripts up and running as quickly as possible.

 A more advanced approach can involve setting up a local Bitcoin Node, as described in *Chapter 5, Installing a Bitcoin Node*, for querying blockchain information. The node can be configured to run as a local service to provide access to real-time transactions and balances.

To start, we're going to use another module. To enhance our script's usability, we'll install `cli-prompt` to make entering information from the command line easier:

```
~ npm install cli-prompt
```

Create a file named `check-balance.js` in your workspace folder and save the following script:

```
// check-balance.js
// Query blockchain.info API to get address balances
var prompt = require('cli-prompt');
```

```
var request = require('request');

// convert 'satoshi' to bitcoin value
var satoshiToBTC = function(value) {
  return value * 0.00000001;
}

prompt('Query Bitcoin balance: ', function (address) {
  // query blockchain.info for the address in JSON format
  var url = "https://blockchain.info/address/" + address +
    "?format=json";
  request(url, function (error, response, body) {
    // check the results of the HTTP call
    if (!error && response.statusCode == 200) {
      // parse the JSON results
      var result = JSON.parse(body);
      // display the results to the console
      // NOTE: results are in 'satoshis' and need to be converted
        to BTC
      console.log('Received: ' +
        satoshiToBTC(result.total_received));
      console.log('Sent: ' + satoshiToBTC(result.total_sent));

      console.log('Balance: ' +
        satoshiToBTC(result.final_balance));
    } else {
      // handle the error
      console.log("Unable to find address");
      if (error)
        console.log("ERROR:", error);
    }
  });
});
```

After saving the files to our work folder, we can run the following script:

```
~ node check-balance.js
Query Bitcoin balance:17x23dNjXJLzGMev6R63uyRhMWP1VHawKc
Received: 50
Sent: 0
Balance: 50
```

In the script, we use `cli-prompt` to allow the user to type or paste a Bitcoin address. The function returns the address as a variable that is then used to query `Blockchain.info`. If the address is found, the result is passed back to us as a JSON object containing the following data:

```
{
    "address": "17x23dNjXJLzGMev6R63uyRhMWP1VHawKc",
    "final_balance": 5000000000,
    "hash160": "4c388152d1d380947df48121d189709b43ea3d01",
    "n_tx": 1,
    "total_received": 5000000000,
    "total_sent": 0,
    "txs": [{
      "block_height": 30,
      "hash": "f5e26c8b82401c…",
      "inputs": [{
        "script": "04ffff001d0121",
        "sequence": 4294967295
      }],
      "lock_time": 0,
      "out": [{
        "addr": "17x23dNjXJLzGMev6R63uyRhMWP1VHawKc","n": 0,
        "script": "41042cf59fafd08…",
        "spent": false,
        "tx_index": 14884,
        "type": 0,
        "value": 5000000000
      }],
      "relayed_by": "0.0.0.0",
      "result": 0,
      "size": 134,
      "time": 1231602122,
      "tx_index": 14884,
      "ver": 1,
      "vin_sz": 1,
      "vout_sz": 1
    }]
}
```

Note how Blockchain.info returns the balance in Satoshis, the smallest Bitcoin unit. In our script, we use the function `satoshiToBTC` to multiply the balance by 0.00000001 to display in units of BTC. Often when working with code, whole numbers are more precise, as the decimal point arithmetic can often lead to rounding errors.

As whole numbers are used on the blockchain, it's recommended to keep to whole numbers throughout your code. Then, when ready to display the value to the user, convert the whole number to the unit of choice: BTC, mBTC, satoshis, and so on.

# Generating addresses for a website

Automating the process of generating addresses and checking balances makes it easy to setup a payment system for a website. A developer can easily pre-generate a list of private keys offline. Then, the developer can upload the corresponding list of public addresses to a web server to collect the payments.

Without the private keys online, the developer can be certain that the money can't be stolen if the server were to be compromised. In the worst case scenario, the hacker can extract a list of the public addresses that only reveal the public balances.

Each order can be assigned a unique address from the pool. Using an automated script, the developer can continuously check for the payments. If a payment has been made in full, the script can then trigger an event to process, ship, and order.

A more advanced system can implement **Hierarchical Deterministic Wallets**, which use a master key to produce an unlimited number of private keys and addresses. The wallet can be arranged to only compute the public addresses while the private keys are stored offline.

# Sending transactions

In *Chapter 5, Installing a Bitcoin Node*, we used the Bitcoin node to build, sign, and broadcast a Bitcoin transaction using the `createrawtransaction`, `signrawtransaction`, and `sendrawtransaction` commands.

In this example, we'll perform the same operations but using Javascript and the BitcoinJS library. The process involves the same three steps:

1. Build a transaction with a list of inputs and outputs.
2. Sign the transaction with the required private keys.
3. Broadcast the transaction to the network.

# Simple transactions

Using the `bitcoinjs` library, we will work with the `TransactionBuilder` object to construct a new transaction. We simply provide the object with one or more private keys as the source of our funds and with one or more addresses for the output, each with the amount we want to send.

 For the following examples, real bitcoin can be at stake. Make sure to have backups of your keys before experimenting with them.

In the following example, our script will prompt for the private key of the source address. The script will then compute the public address, query Blockchain.info for the amount, and write a Bitcoin transaction for us to confirm. A small transaction fee that will be paid to the miner will be included in the transaction. To include this fee, it is simply deducted from the total amount we want to send.

 To improve clarity in the examples, we'll truncate the digits of long keys, addresses, and hashes.

```
// send-transaction.js
// Create and send a Bitcoin transaction
// 1 - query for unspent outputs
// 2 - create a transaction
// 3 - forward the transaction to the network

var bitcoin = require('bitcoinjs-lib');
var request = require('request');
var prompt = require('cli-prompt');

// convert 'satoshi' to bitcoin value
var satoshiToBTC = function(value) {
    return value * 0.00000001;
};

// broadcasts a transaction to the network via blockchain.info
var broadcast_tx = function(tx) {
  var options = {
    url: "https://blockchain.info/pushtx",
     formData: {
      tx: tx.toHex()
     }
    };
```

```
    request.post(options, function(err, httpResponse, body) {
      if (err) {
        console.error('Request failed:', err);
      } else {
        console.log('Broadcast results:', body);
        console.log("Transaction send with hash:", tx.getId());
      }
    });
  }


// fee to pay the miners
var tx_fee = 10000;


// prompt for the private key of the source address
prompt('Enter the private key of the source address (WIF format): ',
function (private_wif) {

  // get the source bitcoin address from the private key
  var private_key = bitcoin.ECKey.fromWIF(private_wif);
  var source_address = private_key.pub.getAddress().toString();

  // query blockchain.info for the unspent outputs from the source
    address
  var url = "https://blockchain.info/unspent?active=" +
    source_address;
  request(url, function (error, response, body) {
    if (!error && response.statusCode == 200) {
      // parse the response and get the first unspent output
      var json = JSON.parse(body);
      var unspent = json["unspent_outputs"][0];

      // prompt for the destination address
      console.log("Found an unspent transaction output with",
        satoshiToBTC(unspent.value), "BTC.");
      prompt('Enter a destination address: ', function
        (dest_address) {

        // calculate the withdraw amount minus the tx fee
        var withdraw_amount = unspent.value - tx_fee;

        // build a transaction
        var txb = new
          bitcoin.TransactionBuilder(bitcoin.networks.bitcoin);
        txb.addInput(unspent.tx_hash_big_endian,
          unspent.tx_output_n);
```

```
        txb.addOutput(dest_address, withdraw_amount);
        txb.sign(0, private_key);
        var tx = txb.build();

        // prompt to confirm sending the transaction
        var confirm = "Send " + satoshiToBTC(withdraw_amount) + "
          plus miner fee? (y/N):";
        prompt(confirm, function(result) {
          if (result.toUpperCase() == "Y") {
            broadcast_tx(tx);
          };
        });
      });
    } else {
      console.log("Unable to find any unspent transaction
        outputs.");
      if (error)
        console.log("ERROR:", error);
    }
  });
});
```

Given everything checks out, the script will build, sign, and broadcast the transaction. The transaction's hash is then logged to the console:

```
~ node send-transaction.js
Enter the private key of the source address (WIF format): L2MswPx…
Found an unspent transaction output with 0.0007 BTC.
Enter a destination address: 1A7L2B9ZnJR…
Send 0.02 plus miner fee? (y/N):y
Broadcast results: Transaction Submitted

Transaction send with hash:02c50c5233dcc01d999…
```

Using the web interface in Blockchain.info, we can then enter the transaction hash displayed at the end of the script to verify that the transaction was indeed broadcasted to the network. The transaction hash can be used as a reliable unique identifier for the transaction.

 Your private keys are never sent to Blockchain.info or the network. The keys are only used locally to digitally sign the transaction.

# Building an Escrow contract

Now that we've illustrated some ways in which we can program Bitcoin, let's apply it to a common example in the real world.

When buying and selling goods over the internet, the two parties involved may choose to exchange the payment through an Escrow account. The purpose of the account is to hold the payment until the item is delivered as agreed. If there is a dispute, a refund is requested or a moderator is introduced to resolve the issue.

Using the Blockchain, we can build a solution that empowers each party with a private key. A multi-signature address is created to hold the payment without the need for a third party to hold the funds. To generate the address, three keys are issued, one each to the buyer, the seller, and the moderator. Of the keys issued, two are required to release the payment.

Given the item is delivered as agreed, the seller generates a withdraw transaction and sends it to the buyer for the first signature. The buyer signs the transaction and returns it to the seller. The seller then signs the withdraw, providing the second signature required, and broadcasts the withdraw to the network for access to the funds.

In the case of a refund, the process is reversed. The buyer creates a refund transaction and requests the seller to sign it. In the case of a dispute, or one party's absence, a trusted moderator holding the third key can aid in resolving the issue with the ability to provide the second signature.

There are advantages to a Blockchain-based escrow. The funds are safely stored in an escrow address rather than in a third-party account. Thus, it's harder for the funds to be compromised. With a Blockchain contract, each party is in control of their portion of the contract.

In addition, the merchant can save on fees, withdraw limits, and delays. Contracts executed on the Blockchain only require a minimal miner's fee, which in today's transactions is usually only a few cents.

Let's begin with an overview of how to implement this system by reviewing the steps involved:

1. Each party generates a private/public key pair. The private key is kept secret and used to sign a withdraw transaction.

2. The buyer collects the public key from each participant and generates a multi-signature Bitcoin address. The address is reproducible for verification purposes.

3. The buyer sends the payment to the address. Each participant can verify the payment on the blockchain. Once the payment is sent to the escrow address, two keys are required to release it.

4. The seller delivers the product and this is confirmed by all the parties involved.

5. The seller generates a withdraw transaction, requiring two of the three signatures. The transaction is sent to the buyer for signing.

6. The buyer signs the transaction and returns it to the seller.

7. The seller then signs the transaction, satisfying the second signature requirement, and broadcasts it to the network.

To implement the system, we'll write a set of scripts that will perform each of these steps for us. For this example, we'll execute the scripts locally on our computer to understand the process. In a real-world example, these scripts could be shared between all the parties or replaced with a more user-friendly system.

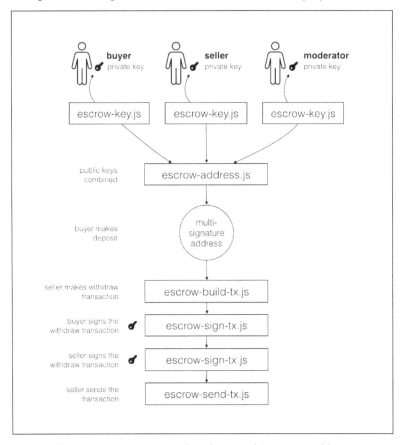

Figure 7.2 - Escrow contract based on a multi-signature address

Figure 7.2 illustrates how the scripts are arranged in the system. The best-case scenario is shown in the illustration, where the buyer releases the payment to the seller, but the system can be slightly modified to issue a refund payment or an override by the moderator.

Now with the system defined, let's begin writing our scripts.

# Generating the keys

For each participant, we'll generate a private/public key pair. Using the functions described earlier in the chapter, we'll generate two files, one containing the public/private keys and the other without the private key.

Create a new script named `escrow-key.js` and save it with the follow script:

```
// escrow-key.js
// generates a random private/public key and address

var bitcoin = require('bitcoinjs-lib');
var fs = require('fs');

// create a new random key
var privKey = bitcoin.ECKey.makeRandom();

// save it in a JSON object to be written to disk
var key_info = {
  private_key: privKey.toWIF(),
  public_key: privKey.pub.toHex(),
  address: privKey.pub.getAddress().toString()
}

// display the key details to the console
console.log("A new private key has been generated for you\n");
console.log("private key:", key_info.private_key);
console.log("public key:", key_info.public_key);
console.log("public address:", key_info.address);
console.log("\n");

// write the key info to disk for backup
var priv_file = "./key-private-" + key_info.address.substring(0,6)
  + ".json";
fs.writeFile(priv_file, JSON.stringify(key_info, null, 4),
  function(err) {
  if (err) { return console.log(err) }
```

```
      console.log("Private key saved as:", priv_file);
  })

  // write public key and address to disk for sharing
  delete key_info["private_key"];  // hide private key
  var pub_file = "./key-public-" + key_info.address.substring(0,6) +
    ".json";
  fs.writeFile(pub_file, JSON.stringify(key_info, null, 4),
    function(err) {
    if (err) {return console.log(err) }
    console.log("Public key saved as:", pub_file);
  })
```

To run the script, we simply execute:

```
~ node escrow-key.js
A new private key has been generated for you

private key: KxfncWVpwmq....
public key: 03b0835dd022ed....
public address: 12xfRFqThM4.....

Public key information saved as: ./key-public-12xfRF.json
Private key information saved as: ./key-private-12xfRF.json
```

The script generates a random private key, and computes the public key and the Bitcoin address from it. Two files are created in the folder and named using the first six characters of the Bitcoin address.

Each user will share the file named key-public-xxxxxx.json with the buyer. Saving the keys in JSON format makes it easy to share and load with Javascript.

The public file contains the public key which is used to generate the multi-signature address. The public key, unlike the Bitcoin address generated from it, does not have any error checking. Any errors made to the string will not be detected. Make sure you handle this with care when sharing.

# Generating the Escrow address

The escrow address is a special type of Bitcoin address that's generated from a list of public keys. Assuming we've collected the public keys from each participant, we can combine them using another script.

Create a new file named `escrow-address.js` and save the following script:

```
// escrow-address.js
// generate a 2-of-3 multi-signature Bitcoin address

var bitcoin = require('bitcoinjs-lib');
var prompt = require('cli-prompt');
var fs = require('fs');

// prompt for the 3 keys
console.log("Create a new escrow address from the public keys of
  each participant.");
prompt.multi([{ key: "buyer" },{ key: "seller" },{ key:
  "moderator" }], function (result) {

  // create a eliptic curve public key from the hex codes
  var pubKeys = [
    bitcoin.ECPubKey.fromHex(result.buyer),
    bitcoin.ECPubKey.fromHex(result.seller),
    bitcoin.ECPubKey.fromHex(result.moderator),
  ]

  // generate a m-of-n multisignature output script
  var redeemScript = bitcoin.scripts.multisigOutput(2, pubKeys);
  var scriptPubKey =
    bitcoin.scripts.scriptHashOutput(redeemScript.getHash());

  // generate the escrow bitcoin address and redeem script
  // stored in a JSON file for organizing the subsequent steps
  var escrow_info = {
    address:
      bitcoin.Address.fromOutputScript(scriptPubKey).toString(),
    redeem_script: redeemScript.toHex().toString()
  }

  console.log("\n");
  console.log("The address to your escrow:", escrow_info.address);
```

```
    // write the escrow info to disk for building a transaction
    var filename = "./escrow-" + escrow_info.address.substring(0,6)
       + ".json"
    fs.writeFile(filename, JSON.stringify(escrow_info, null, 4),
       function(err) {
    if (err) {return console.log(err) }
    console.log("Escrow information saved as:", filename);
    })
  });
```

In this preceding script, we prompt the user to provide us with the three public keys from each user. We then generate a public key object from the hex codes. Using the `bitcoin.scripts.multisigOutput` function, we create a Bitcoin script that requires two of the keys from the list to spend. From this script, we create the hash that is used to generate our address using `bitcoin.scripts.scriptHashOutput`.

We then store the address and the redeem script, in hexadecimal format, as a JSON object and save it to disk:

```
~ node escrow-address.js
Create a new escrow address from the public keys of each participant.
buyer: 03768c29a9…
seller: 036a110b3c…
moderator: 02f38df7cc…

The address to your escrow: 3Ci6QdGyPF…
Escrow information saved as: ./escrow-3Ci6Qd.json
```

The Bitcoin address is used to receive and lock the payment. This address is publicly accessible from the blockchain and can be used to verify that a payment has been made.

 Multisignature Bitcoin addresses start with a 3.

At this point, the buyer can send the payment to the address. When confirmed, the seller can make arrangements to deliver the item.

In the next step, we'll use the redeem script to generate a withdraw transaction.

# Creating a withdraw script

Assuming the item was delivered as agreed and all the parties are happy, we can take the next step and create a withdraw transaction for the seller. The transaction will specify where the funds will be sent and the amount to send. To keep the example simple, we'll withdraw the full amount to one address.

Create a new file named `escrow-build-tx.js` and save the following script:

```
// escrow-build-tx.js
// Create a transaction to withdraw the escrow balance

var bitcoin = require('bitcoinjs-lib');
var request = require('request');
var prompt = require('cli-prompt');
var fs = require('fs');

// fee to pay the miners
var tx_fee = 10000;

// convert 'satoshi' to bitcoin value
var satoshiToBTC = function(value) {
  return value * 0.00000001;
}

// load the escrow json file
var escrow_filename = process.argv[2];
if (!escrow_filename) {
  console.log("Please provide the escrow filename.")
  console.log("example usage: node escrow-build-tx.js ./escrow-
    3Bh334.json")
  return;
}
var escrow = require(escrow_filename);

console.log("Create a withdraw transaction for the escrow
  address:", escrow.address);
prompt('Choose a bitcoin address to send the balance: ', function
  (address) {

  // query blockchain.info for the unspent outputs from the escrow
    address
  var url = "https://blockchain.info/unspent?active=" +
    escrow.address;
  request(url, function (error, response, body) {
    if (!error && response.statusCode == 200) {
```

```
        // parse the response and get the first unpsent output
        var json = JSON.parse(body);
        var unspent = json["unspent_outputs"][0];

        // calculate the withdraw amount minus the tx fee
        var withdraw_amount = unspent.value - tx_fee;

        // build a transaction
        var txb = new
          bitcoin.TransactionBuilder(bitcoin.networks.bitcoin);
        var redeem_script =
          bitcoin.Script.fromHex(escrow.redeem_script);
        txb.addInput(unspent.tx_hash_big_endian,
          unspent.tx_output_n, bitcoin.Transaction.DEFAULT_SEQUENCE,
            redeem_script);
        txb.addOutput(address, withdraw_amount);
        var tx = txb.buildIncomplete();

        console.log("Unsigned transaction created to withdraw",
          satoshiToBTC(withdraw_amount), "BTC with",
            satoshiToBTC(tx_fee), "BTC mining fee.");

        // save the unsigned transaction as json to disk
        escrow.signatures_required = 2;
        escrow.signatures = 0;
        escrow.pay_to_address = address;
        escrow.amount = withdraw_amount;
        escrow.fee = tx_fee;
        escrow.encoded_tx = tx.toHex();

        // write the json to disk
        fs.writeFile(escrow_filename, JSON.stringify(escrow, null,
          4), function(err) {
          if (err) { return console.log(err) }
          console.log(escrow_filename, "has been updated with the
            withdraw transaction.")

        });

      } else {
        console.log("Unable to get an unspent transaction output.");
        if (error)
          console.log("ERROR:", error);
      }
    });
  })
```

To run the script, we need to provide the name of the file generated by the
`escrow-address.js` script, which contains the redeem script. We load this
file as an argument to the script:

```
~ node escrow-build-tx.js ./escrow-3J2fuD.json
Create a withdraw transaction for the escrow address: 3J2fuD…
Choose a bitcoin address to send the balance: 3KQFR…
Unsigned transaction created to withdraw 0.08 BTC with 0.0001 BTC
mining fee.
./escrow-3J2fuD.json has been updated with the withdraw
transaction.
```

The script looks for the first unspent transaction output and prompts for a
destination address. The amount listed is the full amount for the output minus the
transaction fee. A redeem script and the Bitcoin address with additional details are
stored in the JSON file, as follows:

```
~ cat escrow-3J2fuD.json
{
"address": "3J2fuD…",
"redeem_script": "522102f38d…",
"signatures_required": 2,
"signatures": 0,
"pay_to_address": "1GEpz…",
"amount": 800000,
"fee": 10000
}
```

The actual transfer is encoded and stored in hexadecimal format as `unsigned_hex`.
This code contains the instructions to make the actual transfer. The encoded
transaction will be passed to the buyer and seller for signing.

# Signing the transaction

The next step involves the seller requesting a signature from the buyer. The seller
can send the `escrow-3J2fuD.json` file to the buyer for the signature. Using the next
script, the buyer can use the private key to sign and return the transaction.

Create a file named `escrow-sign-tx.js` and save the following script:

```
// escrow-sign-tx.js
// Sign the escrow transaction with a private key

var bitcoin = require('bitcoinjs-lib');
var prompt = require('cli-prompt');
var fs = require('fs')
```

```
  // convert 'satoshi' to bitcoin value
  var satoshiToBTC = function(value) {
    return value * 0.00000001;
  }


  // load the escrow json file
  var escrow_filename = process.argv[2];
  if (!escrow_filename) {
    console.log("Please provide the escrow filename.")
    console.log("example usage: node escrow-sign-tx.js ./escrow-
      3Bh334.json")
    return;
  }
  var escrow = require(escrow_filename);


  // report the details of the escrow transaction
  console.log("Sign withdraw of", satoshiToBTC(escrow.amount), "BTC
  to", escrow.pay_to_address);
  console.log("Transaction has", escrow.signatures, "of",
  escrow.signatures_required, "signatures");


  // exit if escrow has been signed by two signatures
  if (escrow.signatures >= escrow.signatures_required) {
    console.log("Escrow transaction is ready to broadcast.");
    return;
  }


  prompt('Private key for signing the transaction (WIF format): ',
  function (val) {
    try {
      // create the transaction builder object
      var script = bitcoin.Script.fromHex(escrow.redeem_script);
      var tx = bitcoin.Transaction.fromHex(escrow.encoded_tx);
      var txb = bitcoin.TransactionBuilder.fromTransaction(tx);

      // sign the transaction
      var private_key = bitcoin.ECKey.fromWIF(val);
      txb.sign(0, private_key, script);

      // build the transaction, either first or second signature
      if (escrow.signatures == 0) {
        // record the first signature
        escrow.encoded_tx = txb.buildIncomplete().toHex();
        escrow.signatures = 1
```

```
        console.log("Escrow transaction requires one more
          signature.");
      }
      else {
        // record the second signature
        var tx = txb.build();
        escrow.encoded_tx = tx.toHex();
        escrow.signatures = 2;
        escrow.tx_hash = tx.getId();
        console.log("Escrow transaction is ready to broadcast.");
      }

      // write the signed transaction to disk
      fs.writeFile(escrow_filename, JSON.stringify(escrow, null, 4),
        function(err) {
          if (err) { return console.log(err) }
      });

  } catch(e) {
    console.log("Unable to sign:", e.message);
  }
})
```

This script will be used first by the buyer and then by the seller to sign the transaction. First the buyer will run the following:

```
Sign withdraw of 0.0007 BTC to 1GEpz…
Transaction has 0 of 2 signatures
Private key for signing the transaction (WIF format): KxQV1YmA8i…
Escrow transaction requires one more signature.
```

After the script has been run, the JSON file will be modified to include the signature in the encoded transaction and an increment to the 'signatures' key.

Once signed, the buyer sends the JSON file back to the seller. The seller then signs the transaction with his private key, using the same script:

```
Sign withdraw of 0.0007 BTC to 1GEpz…
Transaction has 1 of 2 signatures
Private key for signing the transaction (WIF format):
KYmAxQV18i…
Escrow transaction is ready to broadcast.
```

The JSON file now contains the fully signed transaction that is ready to broadcast to the network. Also included in the JSON file is the transaction's hash, which can be used as a reference to verify the transmission to the network.

# Broadcasting the transaction

Now we're down to the last step: broadcasting the transaction to the network. Now that our transaction has both the signatures, we can simply call Blockchain.info's API to broadcast the transaction.

Create a new file named `escrow-send-tx.js` and save the following script:

```
// escrow-send-tx.js
// broadcast the signed transaction to the network

var request = require('request');
var fs = require('fs');

// load the escrow json file
var escrow_filename = process.argv[2];
if (!escrow_filename) {
  console.log("Please provide the escrow filename.")
  console.log("example usage: node escrow-sign-tx.js ./escrow-
    3Bh334.json")
  return;
}
var escrow = require(escrow_filename);

// broadcast the encoded transction to the network via
blockchain.info
var options = {
  url:'https://blockchain.info/pushtx',
  formData: {tx:escrow.encoded_tx}
};

request.post(options, function(err, httpResponse, body) {
  if (err) {
    console.error('Request failed:', err);
  } else {
    console.log('Broadcast results:', body);
  }
});
```

The seller, when ready can simply run the script as:

```
~ node escrow-send-tx.js
Broadcast results:  Transaction sent!
```

If successful, the transaction's hash, located in the JSON file, can be used to query Blockchain.info's website for confirmation.

# Refunding

Depending on the outcome of the physical exchange, the participants can agree on who's entitled to the final withdraw by signing the transaction. A buyer can request a refund by sending a withdraw request to the seller asking for his signature. If the seller agrees, the buyer simply signs the withdraw and forwards it back to the buyer.

In the case of a dispute, either party can send the moderator a withdraw request and an audit trail or proof of their claim. Using the third key, the moderator has the ability to grant the withdraw or recommend an alternative resolution.

# Summary

In this chapter, we've demonstrated the power of programmable money and how it can refine and reshape the financial industry. Starting by automating simple Bitcoin operations, we learned how to send and receive money. We closed the chapter with a real-world example by implementing a decentralized escrow contract on top of the blockchain.

An advantage of using cryptographic keys is that it virtually eliminates fraud, and reduces the costs and risks involved.

As demonstrated, using the blockchain to script various contracts is a very powerful tool for creating more efficient and transparent financial services.

In the next chapter, we'll explore alt-coins and look at how we can use digital contacts to implement a voting system using a platform called Counterparty.

# 8

# Exploring Alternative Coins

*"Cryptology represents the future of privacy [and] by implication [it] also represents the future of money, and the future of banking and finance."*

*– Orlin Grabbe, Economist, Prolific Writer*

Bitcoin's success has led to the experimentation and adaptation of its underlying protocols and mechanisms. Since its release, there have been over five hundred alternative coins launched. Each coin assumes the liberty to borrow from and modify Bitcoin to implement its own variations on the original design.

In this chapter, we'll look at four innovative alternate coins (Litecoin, Namecoin, Peercoin, and Primecoin) to see how they have leveraged the blockchain technology to implement various concepts and systems in a decentralized way.

We'll see how the alternative coins can be used to store and validate arbitrary pieces of information such as domain names, public records, and digital assets. By simply changing the parameters of the blockchain, it can be used to arrange various bits of information in a way that is publicly transparent, easy to audit, and protected from manipulation. With these characteristics, developers have the tools necessary to create new and innovative systems.

In this chapter, we'll cover the following topics:

- The Introduction of Litecoin, Namecoin, Peercoin, and Primecoin
- Alternative consensus mechanisms and distribution schemes
- How to evaluate alternative coins
- Protocols built on the Bitcoin Blockchain
- Building a voting system with Counterparty

With so many alternative coins in existence today, how can one determine the legitimacy of a particular coin? How do we examine and compare the technical and economic merit of each coin? How do we leverage an alternative coin's unique implementation?

To answer these questions, let's start by exploring how so many coins came into existence, and more importantly, how we can discern which coins are worthy of interest.

# Open source money

In the previous chapters, we have covered open source and have seen how the developers are able to quickly seed an idea and publish it, so that others can help contribute. The emergent effect is the rapid development of high-quality software. When developers from different backgrounds and perspectives are able to work together, difficult programming challenges are quickly resolved.

Bitcoin was launched as an open source project from the start. Early on, the developers were involved with the bug fixes and improvements. Satoshi Nakamoto was key in planting the seed for Bitcoin, but without a community of developers sharing and reviewing the code, the amount of trust earned by the system would have been limited. The open source approach inspires others to experiment.

Less than 2 years after Bitcoin's launch, the first alternative coin, an alternative test blockchain, appeared. It was called the **Bitcoin Testnet**. Launched in October of 2010, its purpose was to create an independent network and blockchain for testing purposes. The developers could easily obtain the Testnet coins, which were not intended to be worth anything, for the purpose of testing apps.

Yet, shortly after its launch, people were using the Testnet coins as real money. Thus, **Testnet2** was launched by generating a new genesis block. Shortly after, **Testnet3** was launched with some improvements and enhancements for testing.

With the ability to fork Bitcoin's original source code, the developers could quickly and easily start their own alternative coins, or `alt-coins`.

# The rise of the alt-coin

As the interest in Bitcoin increased, the developers started proposing alternative uses for the blockchain technology. Early in 2011, several new alt-coins were launched to demonstrate this potential.

With each alt-coin, the developers imagined alternatives to the underlying mechanisms that make Bitcoin work. Primarily, the alt-coin developers searched for ways to improve the "proof-of-work" consensus system, on which the mining protocols were based, and ways to improve the distribution of coins.

The other alt-coins experimented with the possibilities of using the blockchain technology to build decentralized applications. The applications included decentralized storage, code execution, and identification.

For our examination of alt-coins, we will introduce several long running alt-coins: *Namecoin*, *Litecoin*, *Peercoin*, and *Primecoin*.

# Namecoin

Recognized as the first true alt-coin based on a fork of the Bitcoin source code, Namecoin is an alt-coin that implements extensions in its blockchain to allow the recording of public name information for various applications. The first of these applications was a substitute for the Internet's **domain name system** (**DNS**).

# Decentralized domain name service

The DNS is similar to a large phone book. When you type `google.com` into your Web browser, a request is made to the DNS servers asking to resolve the name to an IP address. The IP addresses are used to route information between two computers on the Internet, similar to the way the telephone system connects two phone numbers together.

With the original DNS system, the centralized authorities had established issue names, such as `google.com` or `wikipedia.org`, to organizations. Once purchased, the organization could modify the list of servers that their domain names resolved to.

There are some controversial issues with relying on central authorities for DNS. In some cases, governments or large corporations can use their power to take over the DNS system. Using their power, they can block, censor, spy, or take over the DNS entries. Free speech advocates claim this abuse of power is unethical, and against the Internet user's right to privacy and the right to access free information.

Namecoin offers a decentralized solution to this problem using blockchain technology. By purchasing namecoins, the users can purchase a .bit domain name by going through a centralized service. With control of their domain name through their private keys, the user can modify or sell the rights to the domain name without intervention.

Because the Namecoin blockchain is decentralized, no entity can compromise the system or block the access. Thousands of nodes, each containing a copy of the Namecoin blockchain, exist to serve and respond to the DNS requests. Without a centralized service to compromise, it becomes very difficult to control and manipulate DNS.

As a real-world example, Namecoins have proven how a decentralized system can replace the centralized organizations on the Internet. In a time of much institutional disruptions, decentralized applications and services may serve as a viable replacement to help preserve the rights of Internet users around the world.

# Merged mining

Namecoin is also recognized as being the first alt-coin to introduce **merged mining**. To explain merged mining, one can recall a computer mining for bitcoins. A new block of transactions is assembled and a cryptographic function is applied to it until a solution to a difficult challenge is found. Once found, the solution is offered to the network as *proof-of-work*. The miners who are the first to submit proof-of-work are aware about new coins.

In most cases, a dedicated miner can only mine one blockchain at a time. However, with the rise of alt-coins, we can have many alternative blockchains competing for this available mining power.

A scenario based on dedicated miners has several effects. First, it creates competition for the miners between blockchains. Furthermore, when trying to launch a new blockchain, such as Namecoin, it could prove difficult to attract a viable number of miners to bootstrap the system. The primary reason being that people don't have an incentive to mine something that is not valuable.

Merged mining allows the proof-of-work from one blockchain to serve as proof-of-work for another as well. In an example between Bitcoin and Namecoin, a miner searching for namecoins can assemble a new block of namecoin transactions and embed a digest of the block into a new block of Bitcoin transactions.

The miner then continues computing the cryptographic function for the Bitcoin block until a valid hash is found for either the Bitcoin difficulty or the Namecoin difficulty.

If the proof-of-work hash is found for the Namecoin blockchain, the Namecoin block and the Bitcoin block are submitted as proof-of-work. The miner is then awarded new namecoins.

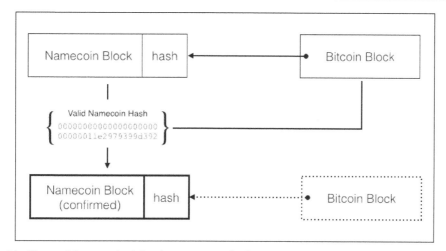

Figure 8.1 - Namecoin's merged mining feature accepts both a Namecoin and Bitcoin block as proof-of-work.

If the valid hash is for the Bitcoin difficulty, the Bitcoin block is submitted as proof-of-work, as normal. Only the hash from the Namecoin block is kept in the Bitcoin block. The miner is then awarded new bitcoins. Ultimately, the mining process remains the same with no changes needed to the protocol to support merged mining.

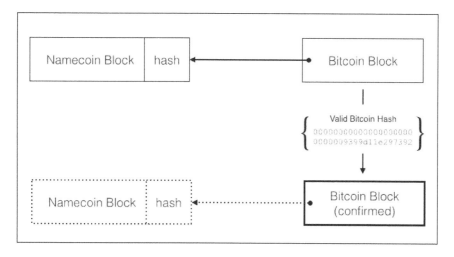

Figure 8.2 - If a valid hash is found for the Bitcoin difficulty, only the hash linked to the Namecoin block is kept.

Lastly, if both are found, then the miner is awarded both bitcoins and namecoins.

Merged mining leverages the same computing power to secure both the blockchains. In our preceding example, Namecoin must be programmed to accept the Bitcoin block as proof-of-work. However, the Bitcoin protocols do not require any changes.

The result is two independent blockchains secured by the same computing power.

 Additional information about the details involved with merged mining is available on the Bitcoin Wiki, at: `https://en.bitcoin.it/wiki/Merged_mining_specification`.

# Litecoin

As the second largest cryptocurrency to date, in terms of market capitalization, Litecoin was built as a clone of the original Bitcoin software. Charlie Lee, an ex-Google employee who is now director of engineering at Coinbase, forked the original Bitcoin-QT code and released it as Litecoin in October of 2011 with some additional changes.

# Block rate

Bitcoin is designed to deliver a new block approximately every 10 minutes. Some had raised the issue that the confirmation time was too long. Thus, Litecoin was launched with an increased block rate approximately every 2 minutes. This gives Litecoin the slight advantage of reducing the confirmation time, which improves the user's experience.

Litecoin can support higher transaction volumes due to the increased number of blocks. A faster block rate also implies that it's harder to double-spend litecoins. As 5 times more Litecoin blocks are produced for every Bitcoin block, the additional confirmations decrease the chances of double-spend.

However, Bitcoin's mining network is much larger and offsets Litecoin's advantage of having a higher block rate. As a disadvantage, the Litecoin network produces a larger blockchain with more orphaned blocks than the Bitcoin network.

The total number of litecoins is fixed at 84 million, 4 times the number of bitcoins. Yet, similar to Bitcoin, the number of litecoins issued through mining rewards halves every four years.

# Scrypt mining

Litecoin's hashing algorithm is based on a different process than Bitcoin's mining algorithm. New blocks in Bitcoin are produced when a miner finds a block with a SHA256 hash that's less than the difficulty hash. On the basis of the varying difficulty level, a miner may need to repeat the hashing function billions of times to find a solution. Thus, the faster a miner can compute hashes, the more chances there are of finding a solution.

Specialized mining equipment, called **Application Specific Integrated Circuits (ASICs)**, have allowed the miners to build high-speed mining rigs, which are able to compute trillions of hashes a second. This has led to a consolidation of the miners, with the side-effect of making the entry into mining impossible for the individual miners.

Litecoin mining is based on a cryptographic function called **scrypt**. Proposed as an alternative to hash mining, it helps to level the playing field for the smaller miners.

Scrypt was designed to make brute force attacks on passwords more difficult. For example, when a user types in a password, a scrypt function is executed to validate the password. This function is designed to use a combination of memory and processing power, which can take several hundred milliseconds to execute. For the user, this happens once each time a password is entered and is negligible.

If an attacker tries to crack the password, he should expect to execute the scrypt function several billions of times to find a solution through brute force. The few hundred milliseconds required for each pass will quickly add up during a brute force attack, making it very difficult to find a solution in any reasonable amount of time.

With Litecoin mining, a scrypt function is used to produce the proof-of-work required to claim a new block and its mining rewards. Because the scrypt function uses a combination of memory and processing power, individual computers are needed. The specialized ASIC mining equipment cannot be generally used to compute the scrypt algorithm.

This approach facilitates the joining of the smaller miners working with individual computers rather than large pools running high performance ASIC chips. This results in a more decentralized mining network.

# Peercoin

Introduced in August 2012, Peercoin is an alt-coin that's mostly based on the original Bitcoin software. Prior to its release, a public announcement was made so that everyone had a fair notice to participate in its public offering. Peercoin's innovative ideas helped increase the energy efficiency of protecting the network with the aim of allowing for greater long-term scalability.

During its launch, new peercoins were issued through a proof-of-work mining process, similar to bitcoins. While the distribution of peercoins is supported through proof-of-work mining, the coins can also be issued through a "minting" process based on an alternative distribution method called **proof-of-stake**.

# Proof-of-stake

Bitcoin's mining process requires a large amount of computing power to generate the proof-of-work needed to create a valid block of confirmed transactions. Designed as an alternative to proof-of-work, the proof-of-stake minting process issues new coins on the basis of the minter's ownership of the existing coins.

In the Peercoin protocol, the ownership of coins is measured by a "coin age". The coin age is calculated by multiplying the owned number of coins with the number of days the coins have been held. To begin competing for a block, a minter must have owned the coins for at least 30 days. Thus, larger and older sets of coins have a greater potential to earn. To offset this, once a set of coins have been used to earn a block, they are reset and 30 days must pass before they are eligible for minting.

Then, the minting process rewards the minters proportionally to the number of coins they own, with a target of 1 percent a year. Unlike Bitcoin's fixed number of coins, peercoins have an annual inflation rate of 1 percent a year.

Compared to Bitcoin's longest running blockchain, the official chain in Peercoin is based on the chain with the highest total consumed coin age.

The end result is a mining system that requires far less computing power than proof-of-work mining. The mining process is also distributed to those who hold the coins rather than to those who own high-performance mining equipment. This further levels the opportunity for entry.

Proof-of-stake is also claimed to be resistant to 51 percent of attacks. As ownership of coins is required for the attack, the cost exponentially increases. Compared with proof-of-work mining, large pools of miners can consolidate to overtake the network.

While the Peercoin network has a technical limit of 2 billion coins, it is only necessary for internal consistency. It is unlikely that the limit will be reached. Additionally, the proof-of-stake inflation rate will continue to produce new coins in the future.

# Primecoin

Introduced in July 2013, Primecoin uses an entirely different method for mining coins. Proof-of-work is presented to the network in the form of prime numbers. Claiming to be the first cryptocurrency designed with scientific computing as its work, the miners compete for primecoins by searching for very large prime numbers.

There is no predefined limit to the number of primecoins, just the natural distribution based on the set of prime numbers. The scarcity of primecoins is set by the distribution of prime numbers within a given set. While each confirmed Bitcoin block contains a nonce and hash solution, each Primecoin block contains a prime number set as the proof-of-work.

Another significant difference between Primecoin and Bitcoin is the mechanism that governs the difficulty level. Rather than using an average block rate calculated after every 2,016 blocks, Primecoin adjusts the difficulty to search for prime number sets after each block with a target rate of one block a minute. Primecoin's quick adjustment interval allows faster confirmation times, approximately 8–10 times faster than Bitcoin.

# Prime numbers

The primary advantage of Primecoin is the usefulness of its proof-of-work to the scientific community. Prime numbers, as most know, are numbers divisible by 1 and itself. Prime numbers have useful applications in the modern-day world, including cryptography. For example, RSA encryption uses large prime numbers to allow two parties to exchange secret messages using two keys, a form of public/private key encryption.

As a general overview, a public key is derived by multiplying two large prime numbers. The private key, which is held secret, is generated from the original two prime numbers. The public key can then be shared to encrypt message that can only be decrypted by the private key.

Alternatively, prime numbers help mathematicians study the distribution of prime number sets. They help answer questions such as "What is the largest gap between two prime numbers?"

# Mining prime numbers

The primecoin network uses three methods to search for prime numbers: Cunningham Chain of the first kind, Cunningham Chain of the second kind, and Bi Twin Chains. Prime number chains are sets of prime numbers with certain mathematical characteristics.

Primecoin mining involves searching for valid sets of a target length. Searching for prime number chains becomes exponentially difficult as the chain's length increases.

Submitted as proof-of-work, it is easy to verify the set using the miners on the network. Because extremely large prime numbers can be hard to verify, there is a maximum size protocol to ensure efficient verification of the sets.

Primecoin miners still create a block of valid transactions to be hashed by SHA256 and include a nonce. This produces a proof-of-work hash similar to Bitcoin. With the hash value, the goal is then to find a valid set of prime numbers. The requirement for the set is that the origin of the chain is a multiple of the proof-of-work certificate.

The difficulty for mining, which is adjusted every block, is based on the length of the chain. Primecoin launched with an initial difficulty level of 7. This means that a chain with 7 primes must be found. Because the difference between a set with 7 and 8 primes can be many times more difficult, a fractional difficulty level is introduced on the basis of a remainder value.

The fractional difficulty level is based on the **Fermat remainder** of the prime number set. For example, with a difficulty of 7.5, approximately half of the chain of length 7 will be valid while the other half will not be.

 While Primecoin is mostly a copy of the Bitcoin software, the mining aspects involve complex mathematical algorithms. If you would like to learn more, download the Primecoin whitepaper from http://primecoin.io/bin/primecoin-paper.pdf.

# Evaluating an alt-coin

With over 500 alt-coins in existence, it's important to be able to discern which are valid and which are scams. Let's look at a few important aspects to consider before buying into an alt-coin.

# Developer activity

As an easy gauge to start with, the developer's activity is helpful when evaluating the legitimacy of a coin. By checking the public repositories of the source code, such as GitHub, one can see when the coin was made public, the contributions made to the code, and the activity level of the community.

As a reference, the GitHub repositories for the alt-coins discussed in this chapter are listed next:

- Litecoin: `https://github.com/litecoin-project`
- Namecoin: `https://github.com/namecoin`
- Peercoin: `https://github.com/ppcoin`
- Primecoin: `https://github.com/primecoin`

Looking through the commits, the developers involved, and the activity over time, one can assess the merits of an alt-coin.

If the source code is not publicly released, it could be a sign of a scam. All legit alt-coins are released as open source. If the developer didn't release the source to the public, it should be seen as a red-flag.

The developer of the coin should also be active on the forums and responsive to questions and comments regarding the coin. If there is no visibility or integration with the public, a red flag should be raised.

Ensure you perform some background checks on the history of the developers and their reputation within the online community.

# Launching of the alt-coin

The method of launching an alt-coin is very important in terms of legitimacy. There should be a prior announcement to the public on forums or in the alt-coin community to give a fair notice to the miners and the users.

There is an instant red-flag if the developer launched the coin after mining the first coins in secret.

Because proof-of-stake requires the holdings of existing coins for minting new coins, a pre-mine action could be taken. This should be openly made public with good reasoning. If there is any inconsistency or shady activity, one should immediately raise a red-flag.

## The legitimate feature set

Without any significant new features or improvements made, an alt-coin could be considered a "copy-cat" scam. Many coins have been introduced just to copy an existing coin with a view to profit. It is advised to avoid these coins.

Additionally, some coins may infringe on the copyrights or trademarks to create hype. Some coins may be named after celebrities and name brands, just to profit from the name. These coins should be avoided as well.

 Exercise caution when getting involved with an alt-coin. Fraudulent IPO, pump-and-dump schemes, and other types of malicious intent are rampant in the alt-coin world. Never send your money to an untrusted exchange or website.

# Protocols built on the Bitcoin Blockchain

Bitcoin's design allows developers to encode small pieces of information into each transaction. Using a predefined protocol, developers are able to build an entirely new alt-coin on top of the existing Bitcoin blockchain.

Several examples of blockchain protocols exist, each with different characteristics. Using these protocols, the developers can define various types of units of accounts, create assets and tokens, and transfer them using standard Bitcoin addresses.

This opens up the blockchain to many useful applications within the business world. As a real world example, the NASDAQ was the first public company to issue private equity using the Colored Coins protocol. With a high level of transparency, the ability to easily audit and resist corruption and manipulation and easily exchange assets using blockchain technology may bring immense value and creditability to the financial world.

## Digital assets

With the ability to issue a unique identifier to the asset, we can issue and track the ownership of any real world property as a *digital asset*. Using public or open sourced protocols, we can easily record the ownership of a digital asset, with its history, on the blockchain.

As an example, the Colored Coins protocol allows the "tagging" of a Bitcoin transaction's output as an issuance of an arbitrary unit. Any subsequent transaction referencing the issuance transaction can then be colored as the unit issued.

Digital assets have many useful cases in the real world. Ownership of physical items, company stocks, or tokens used for voting can be issued, transferred, and audited.

In the next section, we'll explore a protocol called Counterparty that will allow us to issue tokens to create a voting system on top of the Bitcoin network.

# Building a voting system with Counterparty

Counterparty is a protocol built on the Bitcoin blockchain that offers some unique features. With the protocol, the developers can create digital assets, transfer the assets, pay distributions, and execute various smart contracts.

Various use cases for these features include:

- Buying and selling tickets and coupons
- Secured access control
- Betting and gaming
- Proof of publication
- Crowdfunding
- Derivatives
- In-game currencies
- Voting tokens and auditing
- Programmable contracts

Counterparty provides easy to use tools for both developers and non-developers to implement these use cases. In our example, we're going to use Counterparty to create a voting system.

# The XCP alt-coin

Counterparty is powered by its own native currency called **XCP**. Using XCPs, you can pay for the issuance of custom digital assets. One can easily purchase or sell XCPs on public markets. XCPs exchanged on the market carry their own exchange rate. At the time of writing, one bitcoin is worth approximately 250 XCPs.

> **ShapeShift** is a quick and easy way to "convert" one cryptocurrency it to another. Most of the alt-coins covered in this chapter, including XCPs, are available for instant conversion. The service is available at http://shapeshift.io.

XCPs were issued, one time, by "burning" bitcoins. Burning bitcoins is the process of sending bitcoins to an address that can never be used again. Essentially, each bitcoin is sent to an address that was created without a private key. The address can only receive coins; without the private key, the coins can never be sent.

By burning bitcoins in exchange for XCPs, the public can be assured that no one received any privilege or advantage over anyone else. Counterparty termed this process "proof-of-burn". Proof-of-burn helped to establish Counterparty as a legitimate protocol and currency.

[  For your reference, the Counterparty proof-of-burn address is `1CounterpartyXXXXXXXXXXXXXXXUWLpVr`. ]

The proof-of-burn process was opened to the public in January 2014. In exchange for depositing bitcoins, the senders received a fixed amount of XCP. During the process, a total of 2,648,755 XCPs were created. This amount is fixed and no more new XCPs will be created.

XCPs are used in Counterparty to issue new digital assets with a custom name, or to execute programmable contracts. However, in our voting system, we will use a pre-assigned name for our asset to save the fee.

# Creating a voting system

Digital tokens issued through Counterparty can be used to represent votes cast by a panel of judges. In our example, we will set up a scenario of two teams, the *Blue Team* and the *Red Team*.

To keep our example simple, we will assume a panel of 3 judges and one administrator. The administrator will be responsible for issuing 3 digital tokens. The administrator will then send one token to each judge. To receive the token, each judge will need to create a wallet and provide the administrator with its address.

The administrator will then create an address for each team. The address will be used to receive tokens from the judges. The administrator will then publish the address to the panel of judges.

Once the "hypothetical performance" has been delivered, the judges will have the opportunity to vote for either team by sending their token.

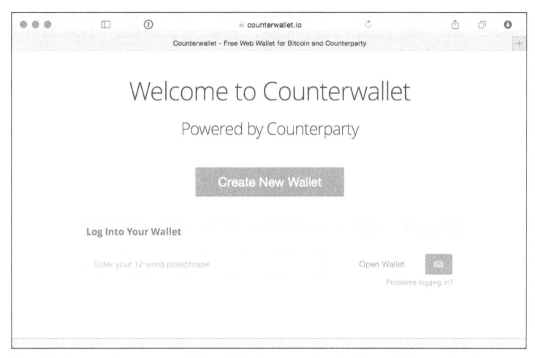

Figure 8.3 - In our voting system, each judge will be given one token. The judges will then use the token to vote for the team of their choice.

To be able to send the tokens, a small bitcoin fee needs to be paid to the network. The miners will collect this fee to confirm the transaction on the Bitcoin network. Once confirmed, the results of the voting system will be final.

Each Counterparty operation will require approximately 0.0005 BTC. In our example, we will need one operation to create the tokens, three operations to issue the tokens to the judges, and three operations for each judge to vote.

With a total of 7 operations, 0.0035 BTC will be needed to fully execute our voting system.

# Creating a wallet

To begin, we'll first need to create a wallet with, in our case, an online service. To simplify our example, we'll use one wallet to hold all the addresses for the administrator, judges, and teams. However, in a real world use case, each participant will be required to create a wallet secured by his own passphrase.

Start by opening the website `http://counterwallet.io` and click on **Create wallet**. The site will generate a 12-word passphrase for you. This passphrase will be used to open and protect your wallet.

Ensure you store this passphrase offline and secure it. If you lose the passphrase, you will not be able to recover it.

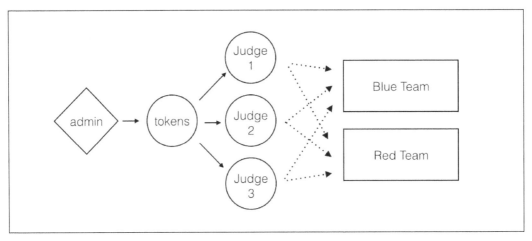

Figure 8.4 - Setting up a new wallet for XCPs using a 12 word passphrase

Once created, your Counterparty wallet will include a new address that you can either use to receive BTC and XCP, or to issue digital assets.

Using the Counterparty protocol, the transfers of digital assets are sent and encoded within the Bitcoin transactions. Thus, the same miners on the Bitcoin network will be confirming your transactions as with normal Bitcoin transactions.

 When issuing, transferring, or sending digital assets, note that the confirmation time, on an average, could take 10 minutes. However, in reality, the actual time needed for a miner to confirm a transaction could vary.

The following screenshot shows a new Counterparty wallet. Your address is displayed with a customizable label. Next to the address, a zero balance is displayed for both BTC and XCP.

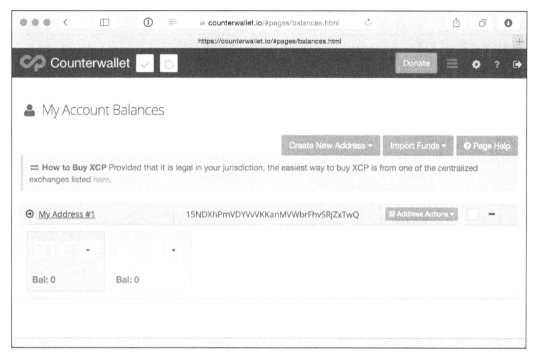

Figure 8.5 - A Counterparty wallet showing a single address and the balance in BTC and XCP.

We'll use the first address for the administrator. Rename the label **My Address #1** to **Administrator** by clicking on the address and entering the name.

Next, we will need to create an address for each judge and team. Simply click on the **Create New Address** button and select **Create Regular Address**. You will be prompted to enter a label.

Proceed by creating a new address for each of the following labels:

- Judge 1
- Judge 2
- Judge 3
- Red Team
- Blue Team

When finished, your wallet should have a total of 6 addresses, each with a zero balance.

# Funding the wallet

Next, we need to fund the administrator with enough BTC to execute four operations. We'll estimate the cost at 0.0005 BTC per operation. The actual amount will likely be less, but having a little extra will give us some wiggle room. At any time of the exercise, you can withdraw the balance, minus any fees paid to the network.

Assuming you have a wallet setup with BTC from earlier in the book, send exactly 0.0020 BTC (0.0005 BTC times 4) to the administrator's address. You can display the QR code or copy the address by clicking on the **Address Actions** button from the panel and selecting **Show QR Code**.

We will need to repeat the funding process for each judge. One operation will be required from each judge to cast their vote. Similar to the case with the administrator, use your bitcoin wallet to send 0.0005 BTC to the address listed for each judge.

Now we will give the network some time to confirm the transactions. After a while the balances of each address will be updated to reflect the deposit. The reflected bitcoin balances should be as follows:

- Administrator: 0.0020 BTC
- Judge 1: 0.0005 BTC
- Judge 2: 0.0005 BTC
- Judge 3: 0.0005 BTC

The following screenshot shows the wallet funded and ready. To improve the readability of the wallet, you can choose to collapse each panel by clicking the "-" button on the right side.

Note that, if you would like to withdraw your deposit, click on the down arrow on the BTC balance and select **Send**. You will be prompted to enter a Bitcoin address and amount.

When the balances are available, we'll be ready to move on to the next step.

Figure 8.6 - The wallet with the administrator and each judge funded.

# Creating the tokens

The next step will be for the administrator to create a digital asset to represent the three tokens. Once created, we will send one token to each of the judges.

To start, click on **Address Actions** and select **Create (issue) a Token**. The dialog box shown in the following screenshot will be displayed.

Ensure **Free numeric name** is chosen for our example. If the address contains an XCP balance, you will have the option of choosing an alpha-numeric name for the asset.

With the **Free numeric name** option selected, Counterparty will generate a random token name for you.

For the description, you can provide any name you want; this is optional.

For the quantity, select exactly 3, one for each of the judges.

Finally, ensure **Make divisible?** is unchecked. Since a vote cannot be divided, we will disable fractions when transferring the units.

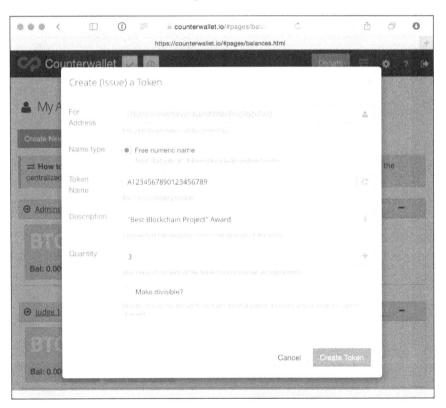

Figure 8.7 - A dialog showing the parameters for our digital asset.

When finished, click **Create Token**. A new transaction, containing information about our digital asset, will be sent to the network for confirmation.

Allow a few minutes for the network to confirm the transaction. Once confirmed, a panel will appear, displaying the identifier and the quantity of tokens available in your digital asset.

Figure 8.8 - The administrator's address listing the issuance of 3 tokens

# Sending tokens

Now that our tokens have been issued, we'll send one to each judge. By sending a token, a transaction will be created on the Bitcoin blockchain containing the details of the transfer.

First, select the address from **Judge 1** by clicking on **Address Actions** next to its address and select **Show QR code**. Copy the address to the clipboard.

Next, click the down arrow in the asset panel, listed in the Administrator address, and select **Send**. You will be prompted with a dialog box as shown in the following screenshot:

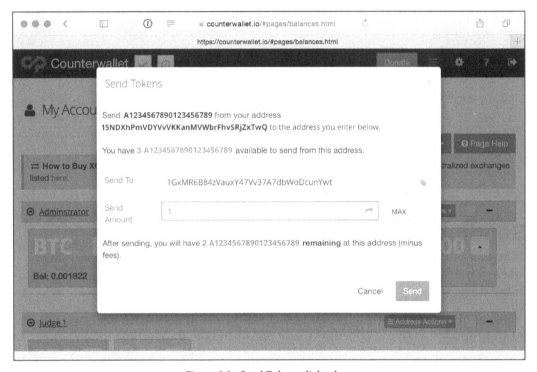

Figure 8.9 - Send Tokens dialog box

Simply paste the address in the **Send To** field, specify the amount as 1, and click on **Send**.

A transaction with the transfer details will be posted to the network, and within a few minutes, the balance will appear under the address for **Judge 1**.

Finish the process by sending exactly one token each to the remaining two judges. At the end of the process, the administrator's balance should be zero and each judge should have exactly one token.

Figure 8.10 - Judge 1 has received the transfer of one token

# Casting votes

Now the stage is set for the final vote! Each judge has been issued with one token representing one vote, and our teams, the Red Team and the Blue Team, are ready to deliver their performance.

 To add a little randomness to the exercise, we can flip a penny for each judge's vote: Heads for the Red Team and tails for the Blue Team.

Each judge will now cast his vote by sending his token to one of the two teams. In our example, our two teams have the following addresses:

- **Red Team**: 1CH9ox9VgZf5DjRzvzL1nbJCZjsAuGoLvX
- **Blue Team**: 1HzVAjrUGMfH9QyT6nFYvkMJ5UnshkB9f7

In the same manner that we issued tokens to each judge, simply have each judge send his token to the address corresponding to the team of his choice.

After each judge sends his token, the public will have cryptographic proof of each vote and a public audit trail for verifying the results. In a real world example, we can maintain a database of the transaction IDs posted to the Bitcoin network, or rely on another service to query the results.

# Verifying the results

We can use a third-party tool called **Blockscan** to verify the results. Blockscan is a service that maintains a searchable index of all the Counterparty assets and transactions. The site "crawls" the Bitcoin blockchain, in real time, and publishes the Counterparty data in an easy to use website.

With a quick search, we can locate our asset and publish a list of the holders of our digital asset.

Open the website `http://blockscan.com` and enter the asset's ID in the search box displayed on the top right. From the results listed, select the asset and click on the **AssetHolders** tab.

The final results are displayed as shown in the following screenshot:

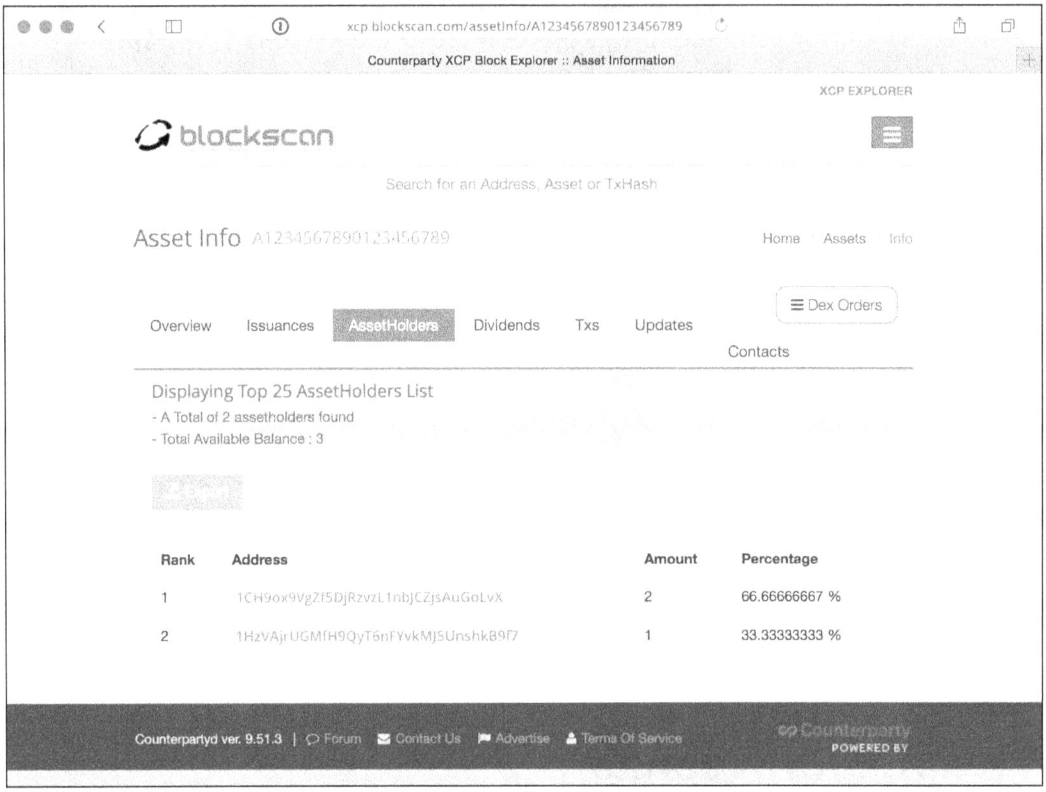

Figure 8.11 - Using Blockscan to display the results of our voting system

In addition to the asset holders, Blockscan provides reports of issuance, transaction history, and, if provided, title information about the assets.

# Finishing up

If we choose, we can continue the voting process as described earlier for additional rounds. Simply repeat the process of issuing another digital asset for the second round, send one to each judge, and allow them to cast their votes.

When finished with the voting process, the BTC balances remaining in each address can be returned to the administrator's wallet.

In a real world system, a team of developers could set up a user-friendly portal for each judge and team to register and a database to hold the addresses representing each participant. The system could then have a fully automated administration process to issue the tokens and assign one to each judge.

Furthermore, the voting process could implement a simple to use interface for casting the votes and a well-formatted public page showing the results in real time.

As exemplified by our voting system, protocols such as Counterparty could be implemented for other uses such as issuing company stock, paying dividends to each shareholder based on the percentage owned, and providing real-time auditing and updates to the public.

Our voting system is one example of many, but as one can imagine, the possibilities from the Blockchain to serve our society are truly endless!

# The future of finance

Looking back in history, technology has changed the world in profound ways. From the steam engine, to computers, to the Internet, we have seen amazing advances in how we can innovate through technology. In line with the previous advances of technology, Bitcoin has the potential to bring the same scale of change to finance.

Since its launch, just months after the financial crises of 2008, Bitcoin has challenged the way we look at money and finance. Consequently, our previous notions of relying on centralized institutions to issue, store, and transfer money are now questionable.

On the basis of what we've seen from the implementation of new technologies since the industrial revolution, many of our financial institutions face major disruption. The Blockchain's distributed ledger has demonstrated its ability to replace many of the functions they currently service. Yet, to our benefit, as Blockchain's adoption increases, we can expect to see more transparency and credibility on a global scale.

We started the book with a gentle introduction to Bitcoin and how to purchase them within 15 minutes. Helping to understand the basics raises awareness of the responsibility that will be assumed when working with crypto-currencies.

Throughout the book, we explained the mechanism behind the functionality of the Blockchain. As a fundamentally new technology, the algorithms that govern the protocol bring together economic, cryptographic, and social curves to support a self-sustaining system. Most impressive is its ability to be exempted from the corruption we often see with centralized power.

Finally, we ended with examples of how it can be extended with alt-coins and how it can be used in various real world applications. The possibilities with Blockchain technology and how it can be adapted are truly endless. Although anyone can start a new alt-coin today, only those that bring true value to the market will succeed.

Today we have front-row seats to a historic transformation. Each one of us plays an active role in this transformation by our choices and actions; as a collective, we can shape the system to empower every individual. Presently, we have the power to improve conditions for economic globalization for us today and tomorrow for future generations.

May the future of finance ultimately serve humanity and the planet it depends on!

# Index

## A

**Alitin Mint**
  URL 49
**alt-coin**
  about 181, 188
  developer activity 189
  evaluating 188
  launching 189
  legitimate feature set 190
**alternative coins**
  about 101
  Friecoin 101
  Litecoin 101
  Namecoin 101
**Antpool**
  URL 146
**ANXPRO**
  URL 43
**Application Specific Integrated Chips (ASICs) 185**
**asymmetric cryptographic algorithm 84**

## B

**balances**
  finding 112
**BFGMiner**
  reference link 145
**BitAddress**
  URL 60
**bitcoin**
  access, verifying to private key 74, 75
  brainwallets 61
  brainwallet security, increasing 63
  cold storage 72
  cold storage, with Electrum 72, 73
  HD wallet, installing 70, 71
  hot wallet 72
  in cold storage 71, 72
  paper wallets 53
  receiving 10, 14
  savings 53
  sending 10-12
  storing 52
  trading, on exchange 43
  used, for housekeeping 75, 76
**Bitcoin**
  about 103
  balance, viewing at 7-9
  charts, reference link 29
  mining 128
  price volatility 27, 28
  programming operations 156, 157
  URL 107
  wiki 144
**Bitcoin addresses**
  cryptographic hashes 86
  explaining 9, 10
  generating 87, 88
  working with 118-120
**Bitcoin blockchain**
  digital assets 190
  protocols 190
**Bitcoin Core**
  about 103-105
  URL, for source code 104
**BitcoinCZ**
  URL 146
**bitcoind 104, 115**

## V

## W

## X

## Thank you for buying
# Learning Bitcoin

# About Packt Publishing

Packt, pronounced 'packed', published its first book, *Mastering phpMyAdmin for Effective MySQL Management*, in April 2004, and subsequently continued to specialize in publishing highly focused books on specific technologies and solutions.

Our books and publications share the experiences of your fellow IT professionals in adapting and customizing today's systems, applications, and frameworks. Our solution-based books give you the knowledge and power to customize the software and technologies you're using to get the job done. Packt books are more specific and less general than the IT books you have seen in the past. Our unique business model allows us to bring you more focused information, giving you more of what you need to know, and less of what you don't.

Packt is a modern yet unique publishing company that focuses on producing quality, cutting-edge books for communities of developers, administrators, and newbies alike. For more information, please visit our website at www.packtpub.com.

# About Packt Open Source

In 2010, Packt launched two new brands, Packt Open Source and Packt Enterprise, in order to continue its focus on specialization. This book is part of the Packt Open Source brand, home to books published on software built around open source licenses, and offering information to anybody from advanced developers to budding web designers. The Open Source brand also runs Packt's Open Source Royalty Scheme, by which Packt gives a royalty to each open source project about whose software a book is sold.

# Writing for Packt

We welcome all inquiries from people who are interested in authoring. Book proposals should be sent to author@packtpub.com. If your book idea is still at an early stage and you would like to discuss it first before writing a formal book proposal, then please contact us; one of our commissioning editors will get in touch with you.

We're not just looking for published authors; if you have strong technical skills but no writing experience, our experienced editors can help you develop a writing career, or simply get some additional reward for your expertise.

Building E-commerce Sites
with VirtueMart Cookbook

Over 90 recipes to help you build an attractive, profitable,
and fully-featured e-commerce store with VirtueMart

John Horton

## Building E-commerce Sites with VirtueMart Cookbook

ISBN: 978-1-78216-208-7      Paperback: 310 pages

Over 90 recipes to help you build an attractive, profitable, and fully-featured e-commerce store with VirtueMart

1. Get to grips with VirtueMart and build an attractive store powered by Joomla!

2. Increase the visibility of your store with SEO and product descriptions.

3. Keep your store profitable by configuring tax, shipping and orders.

Advanced Quantitative
Finance with C++

Create and implement mathematical models in C++ using
Quantitative Finance

Alonso Peña, Ph.D.

## Advanced Quantitative Finance with C++

ISBN: 978-1-78216-722-8      Paperback: 124 pages

Create and implement mathematical models in C++ using quantitative finance

1. Describes the key mathematical models used for price equity, currency, interest rates, and credit derivatives.

2. The complex models are explained step-by-step along with a flow chart of every implementation.

3. Illustrates each asset class with fully solved C++ examples, both basic and advanced, that support and complement the text.

Please check **www.PacktPub.com** for information on our titles

Microsoft Dynamics NAV
Financial Management

Cristina Nicolàs Lorente
Laura Nicolàs Lorente

## Microsoft Dynamics NAV Financial Management

ISBN: 978-1-78217-162-1      Paperback: 134 pages

Delve deep into the world of financial management with Microsoft Dynamics NAV

1. Explore the features inside the sales and purchases areas as well as functionalities including payments, budgets, cash flow, fixed assets, and business intelligence.

2. Discover how the different aspects of Dynamics NAV are related to financial management.

3. Learn how to use reporting tools that will help you to make the right decisions at the right time.

Joomla! E-Commerce
with VirtueMart

Build feature-rich online stores with Joomla! 1.0/1.5 and
VirtueMart 1.1.x

## Joomla! E-Commerce with VirtueMart

ISBN: 978-1-84719-674-3      Paperback: 476 pages

Build feature-rich online stores with Joomla! 1.0/1.5 and VirtueMart 1.1.x

1. Build your own e-commerce web site from scratch by adding features step-by-step to an example e-commerce web site.

2. Configure the shop, build product catalogues, configure user registration settings for VirtueMart to take orders from around the world.

3. Manage customers, orders, and a variety of currencies to provide the best customer service.

Please check **www.PacktPub.com** for information on our titles

www.ingramcontent.com/pod-product-compliance
Lightning Source LLC
Chambersburg PA
CBHW060548060326
40690CB00017B/3639